AMERICAN

REFUGEES

BOOKS

Heir
The Mama Tass Manifesto
The Big Fix
Wild Turkey
Peking Duck
California Roll
The Straight Man
Raising the Dead
The Lost Coast
Director's Cut
Turning Right at Hollywood & Vine
I Know Best
The GOAT

SCREENPLAYS

The Big Fix
Bustin' Loose (story by Richard Pryor)
My Man Adam
Enemies, A Love Story (with Paul Mazursky)
Scenes from a Mall (with Paul Mazursky)
Prague Duet (with Sheryl Longin)
A Better Life (story)

AMERICAN

REFUGEES

THE UNTOLD STORY OF

THE MASS EXODUS FROM

BLUE STATES TO RED STATES

ROGER L. SIMON

Encounter
BOOKS

First American edition published in 2022 by Encounter Books,
an activity of Encounter for Culture and Education, Inc.,
a nonprofit, tax-exempt corporation.
Encounter Books website address: www.encounterbooks.com

Manufactured in the United States and printed on
acid-free paper. The paper used in this publication meets
the minimum requirements of ANSI/NISO Z39.48–1992
(R 1997) (*Permanence of Paper*).

FIRST AMERICAN EDITION

LIBRARY OF CONGRESS
CATALOGING-IN-PUBLICATION DATA
IS AVAILABLE
Information for this title can be found at
the Library of Congress website under
the following ISBN 978-1-64177-397-3.

For Glenn Reynolds,
who had a greater impact on my life
than even he knows.

Wish that I was on ol' Rocky Top
Down in the Tennessee hills
Ain't no smoggy smoke on Rocky Top
Ain't no telephone bills

—Felice and Boudleaux Bryant

CONTENTS

1

A STORY "ROCKY TOP" TOLD ME

I was in the home, some miles south of Nashville, of a man I was told knew as much about the inside of Tennessee politics as anyone.

For anonymity, he is known online as "Rocky Top," after the Osborne Brothers bluegrass hit.

It was our first meeting.

He began by recounting a tale told him by a couple living in Greeneville, Tennessee, population 15,479.

The couple had watched for over a year while a rather elaborate house was being constructed next door without any indication of whose it was. Finally it was completed, and the family arrived. The woman of the new house walked over to introduce herself to the couple that very day.

"We're from California" she said, before adding quickly, "But we're not bringing California values with us...in case you were wondering." ■

2

THE MAKINGS OF
AN AMERICAN REFUGEE

My family and I were less than three hours out of Los Angeles when I thought, What on God's intermittently green earth am I doing? We had stopped for a bite and gas somewhere out in the Mojave at one of those Last Chance Saloon kind of places run by aging hippies, with a store stocked with chimes, ankhs, and peace symbols that seemed to have spiderwebs attached.

Unappealing and dated as this rest stop was, it created a nostalgic feeling in the pit of my stomach, but not the pleasant kind—more like remorse. What, indeed, was I doing? I was betraying my dreams. I was a coward, admitting failure, even if I had had moments of success. Born a New Yorker, I had come to California as a young man of twenty-one for more than just endless summers and ocean waves. I wanted to be part of the film industry, to write and direct movies. And now here I was, in my seventies, running away to start a new life—of what kind and for what purpose?—in Tennessee. I would be the proverbial fish out of water.

But, as the French say, *les jeux sont faits*. The chips were down, and I had placed my bet. I should say *our* bet, including my wife as well as daughter, who was then just shy of her twentieth birthday. This move had originally been their idea. They had worked

3

to persuade me finally to effectuate a change that we had been mulling for over a decade.

At that point (June 1, 2018) we were still somewhere near the beginning of a growing trend of people fleeing blue states for red— moving from California certainly, but other states too, prominently New York and Illinois—a trend that has made the cost of renting a U-Haul prohibitive in Los Angeles but cheap in Sarasota.

Four years later, it hadn't stopped. A 2022 census showed that nearly a quarter of those still streaming into Tennessee were from California. No other state was close. Tennessee's population had grown more than 9 percent in the last decade, with more than a half million new residents moving in.

In 2022, the *Babylon Bee* had some fun with the trend, publishing the satirical listicle "10 Biggest Adjustments Fleeing Californians Have to Make in Their New States." Some of my favorites were "There's no need to call the police if you see someone with a gun strapped to their hip" and "No one cares about your preferred pronoun."

Indeed not, but as funny as their list is, the *Bee* had it dead wrong about the reality of the people exiting California for red states. There's got to be an exception somewhere, but as far as I could tell after four years, there wasn't a "they/them" among them.

These were people looking to return to the America they had grown up in—yearning for it actually, to the extent that they would get up and trek a couple of thousand miles with their families to find it, emulating Steinbeck's Joad family in reverse. They were also, to a great extent, innocents abroad, American refugees in their own land about to engage in a culture clash that would, whether they knew it or not, change the country they loved. Yet they were impelled to go.

Nevertheless, back in 2005, when I was helping found the blog aggregation site Pajamas Media and it became public (once conventionally left-wing, I had moved to the right after September 11),

I still didn't give a thought to leaving. The first wake-up call came a couple of years later, when I received a handwritten note in the mailbox of our Hollywood Hills home. "We know where you live," it said. I never could figure out who wrote it, but it was a harbinger of the radical split in our culture, accompanied by unremitting anger, that we have come to live with. It was also an early influence on my ultimate decision to leave.

The intervening years of hesitant rumination have given me some empathy for and insight into the challenges and difficult decisions faced by many of the people I interviewed or casually spoke with for this book. Moving, uprooting yourself, is not a simple matter. Families can be disrupted, friends and jobs can be lost, and whole habits of life can be upended. Yet many are doing it anyway. The question is, Why?

For me, with the prodding of my wife and daughter, the question became, How could I stay here any longer? After some reluctance, some natural inertia (what were we to do with all those books?), I could not ignore the elephant in the room—or rather, the stampeding herd of elephants, rhinoceroses, and water buffalo.

California was no longer the paradisal land of the Beach Boys it was when everybody I knew wanted to be in LA. The state had evolved into a kind of madhouse of the woke, with people defecating in the streets, homeless encampments lining nearly every freeway underpass, and syringes littering once-magnificent beaches, making you loath to lie down in the sand or even take your shoes off.

Though I was no longer a leftist of any sort by the time we departed—in fact I had come to see leftism, the modern kind anyway, as a rich man's fraud—in those few hours we had driven, I had been replaying in my mind not just the Beach Boys but the lyrics to Woody Guthrie's anthem "Do Re Mi" with its mordantly cynical view of the once-Golden State as an Eden for the rich only, actually now the mega-rich.

It was hard to deny that. California suffered under the stultification of the one-party state, with the rich richer than they had ever been. It was unlikely to change, not in the short run anyway. Woody Guthrie's old Left was long gone, and the "woke" ideology that replaced it had little or nothing to do with the working class. Its adherents seemed even to despise the common man. These days California was ruled by an anti-working-class Left of self-centered, rich elitists. I had to get out of there.

Another verse of Woody's anthem concluded with a recitation of states to which the wise person should return. The last on that list, for rhyming purposes evidently, was Tennessee.

That was where I was going—Tennessee. But I was not going back in any literal sense. I barely knew the place. I had only been there briefly a few times before—once for a tour of Vanderbilt University and twice to house-hunt in Nashville. For the latter we were driven around by a realtor, leaving me—despite the realtor's well-intended efforts—with scant knowledge of exactly where we were, except that we were indeed in Music City. That was Tootsies, the fabled honky-tonk, on our left, she indicated as we passed. I had seen its more recent clone at the airport, filled with passengers awaiting flights while downing local beers and listening to a young girl playing covers of country standards I but vaguely recognized. The crowd seemed to know them well. ■

3

WAS IT IN HOMAGE TO JOHNNY CASH?

We had chosen Nashville because it was a creative place—Music City—with at least that much resemblance to LA. My wife, also a writer, and I felt we needed something familiar, although neither of us had ever written or even seriously contemplated writing a song. We didn't play instruments either. So we looked on in wonder whenever we got on a plane to fly into or out of the city. It seemed as if every fourth passenger was lugging a guitar or struggling to stow one between the carry-ons in the overhead bins. The city's airport resembled an outpost of the Hard Rock Hotel, with gold-plated Gibsons in glass display booths and pictures of Johnny Cash and Dolly Parton smiling at you as you descended to the baggage check. Who needed a governor or a mayor? They were nonentities by comparison.

Still, deep down, I had no real idea why I had chosen Tennessee and not, say, Florida or South Carolina, other than that my wife and daughter favored the former. Had Tennessee, bizarre as it sounds, chosen me? Or maybe it was all random. Regardless, I had had enough of California and needed to get out.

I did, however, have a strange—you might even call it cosmic—connection to Tennessee from when I was about seven years old. In those days, the early 1950s, my father would fly down every month to a place in the eastern part of the state near Knoxville called Oak Ridge. Referred to by some as the Mystery City, Oak Ridge was more accurately the Atomic City: along with Los Alamos, New Mexico, and Hanford, Washington, it was where our country's early nuclear research was conducted. My father, a radiologist, made monthly visits there to give his professional opinion on the possible human outcomes from the latest weapons. This was during the development of the hydrogen bomb and later the neutron bomb, so he invariably returned with a grim expression on his face, as if he had seen several million ghosts. That was my first inkling of the place called Tennessee.

But that was a long time ago, and mostly forgotten. In truth I didn't know much about the state where I was headed. I didn't even know that it was, as Julius Caesar said of Gaul, divided into three parts—Eastern, Middle, and Western Tennessee. I certainly knew little about Nashville, my new home city. And nobody there, as far as I was aware, knew me.

That turned out to be not entirely true. Once there, I discovered that people did know me—from my writing. This was the same writing that had gotten me more or less excommunicated by the Left, had seen me rejected in Hollywood, and would, in the future, have me "canceled" (permanently, apparently) by Facebook, which is actually something of a badge of honor in conservative circles.

Some of these people even sought me out after I arrived in Tennessee. It had caught their eye when I wrote online of my move. Though it was just a few people, I was surprised and relieved. I had lost a number of friends over the years because of that same writing. Nobody loves an apostate. Or, to put it another way, I found out who my friends really were. Most of us don't have that many good friends in the first place, but I lost almost all of the few I had. And here were people welcoming me: one an old member of the Nashville gentry, from a family that had built the city; another an under-the-radar right-wing professor from a local university. I was glad to meet them, and I still count them as friends. Who wants to be alone in a new location, having left a city where they had lived for the better part of fifty years?

Not long after that, and equally to my surprise, I was invited on a local radio show by a man I had employed in Los Angeles some years before for the now-defunct PJTV, an early foray into internet television. I had forgotten that Michael Patrick Leahy came from Nashville and—since his show was in the early morning, starting at 5 a.m., and I am the type who doesn't come to until his fifth cup of coffee—I hadn't listened in. But soon enough I was fighting my constitution, getting up at what I considered the crack of dawn (actually just after 6 a.m., when most working people are long since awake). All this to appear as a regular on his show, broadcasting to my newly adopted city before I really understood much of what was happening there or who the important people were.

I would learn.

So I have written this book because it is my story too. I took the southbound train that the bluegrass band Old Crow Medicine Show memorialized so poignantly in "Wagon Wheel," the song that became the theme, in Darius Rucker's version, of Ken Burns's PBS documentary series on country music. The lyrics were written, in part, by Bob Dylan. Strictly speaking, however, I did not go south or take any southbound train. Nashville is at the same latitude as Los Angeles, even though you wouldn't know it in the dead of winter.

But then again, I really was in the South. Not as far south as Mississippi and Alabama, but close enough. In effect, I was an American refugee, as were so many others heading from blue states like New York, California, and Illinois to red states like Florida, Texas, and Tennessee.

But were we really "refugees" in the true sense of the word, and not just conventional migrants moving across the country, substituting "Southward Ho!" for "Westward Ho!"? I submit that we were and are. Only this time, almost uniquely in American history, especially given the obvious influence on our elections, we have native refugees who are reshaping the country just as conventional foreign refugees did in the past.

I never dreamed I would think of myself as one, yet I do. But then, America was built by refugees—reluctant and otherwise—from the Pilgrims to the Ashkenazi Jewish "greenhorns" of New York's Lower East Side. The list is endless. And all (well, almost all) blended into our country, not only enriching it but finding themselves changed in the process. Sometimes this was turned into the stuff of legend, as we have seen in the *Godfather* films or in the plays of Eugene O'Neill. Would these internal refugees have the same impact? I didn't know back in 2018, but early on I suspected something was happening. I just didn't know what. ∎

4

WHY ARE THESE PEOPLE SO NICE?

I did know that I was definitely in "the South." The folkways were different, as I knew they would be. People, in general, were much nicer. In the first few weeks after my arrival, after so many years in New York and Los Angeles, I even thought such friendly behavior was a trick. Indeed, it sometimes was, as when a lady of a certain age would tell her peer "Bless your heart," seemingly as a compliment but actually to plant an emotional dagger squarely in the other woman's back.

But that was pretty old school—a phrase that, by the time I arrived, was more heard about than heard. By and large, everybody really *was* nice, particularly working-class people—those who fix your plumbing or electricity or whom you meet at the supermarket checkout. These tend to be the nicest people everywhere, but they were more so in the South. Your clerk might even make a special fuss at the checkout counter if he heard you were a newcomer. "Two weeks? Well, welcome. Hope you're likin' it so far. So glad y'all came. If y'all need something, just holler."

A surprising number of people, even college students, still did say "y'all," but fewer with authentic Southern accents. That clerk might have arrived in town only six weeks ago. You would have to check the area code on his cellphone to find out if he's the real deal. It's one thing to move states, and another to change your phone number.

Of course, the worst thing you can do is put on a phony Southern accent like Hillary Clinton. In fact, of the ten longtime Nashvillians I regularly came to play tennis with, only one had a strong traditional Southern accent. At first, I had trouble understanding him; then I came to enjoy, even admire, his more colorful, storytelling way of speaking. I remember learning in college that the pronunciation of Shakespeare's English was said to resemble the Southern accent, which linguists discovered after puns were revealed when the plays were read with a drawl.

Nevertheless, this tennis player with a drawl was a rarity in my world, which tended to be more urban than rural. Metro Nashville—whose center was blue and whose surroundings, like most of Tennessee, were red—was growing at an extraordinary pace, causing many to fear, with justification, that the city would turn into "another Atlanta," as locals darkly put it: Music City without the music, just endless urban sprawl laced with interminable traffic.

And yet this was still, deep down (maybe not so far down), the South—something I came to deem good as far as the people were concerned. Its political leadership would become another question.

I wasn't completely a newcomer to the region. I had been there before, below the Mason-Dixon Line, during the civil rights movement of the sixties, and for the 2016 election. Even before that, for a week or so as an eleven-year-old boy, I visited family friends in Louisiana during Jim Crow, staring in undeserved Northern liberal superiority and contempt at my first "colored only" water fountain. But that was all long gone now. The Nashville Woolworth where the first sit-ins were staged had been turned into a restaurant-cum-museum of the period.

And of course, I knew the South through literature, some of which I loved naturally (Harper Lee) and some of which I did so only with effort (Faulkner). I would try again soon, with more intimate knowledge of the region and its customs.

So my small family was part of a wave, the most recent of many. "Moving on" was always a part of American life, even before the days of Manifest Destiny. "Westward Ho!" was the watchword until we got as far west as we could, and then we started going every which way. Today, that arrow is pointing from blue states to red.

Et Tu, Condé Nast?

This migration, however, was more than a little different from its predecessors. Large numbers of Americans had fled blue states for what were clearly political and cultural reasons. They were tired of governments bent on controlling every aspect of their lives, and they were as sick of the woke as I was—of being called racist, sexist, ageist, ableist, and, inevitably, white supremacist before they even opened their mouths.

And of course they were sick of the COVID-19 mandates that flipped the sixties apothegm "our bodies, ourselves" on its head, making our bodies the slaves of the government and its many corporate collaborators. One such company was the oh-so-trendy Condé Nast, which retained some dwindling cultural clout through legacy magazines such as the *New Yorker* and *Vanity Fair*. Part of that "progressive" influence was decreeing that all their employees had to take the vaccine, whether or not they worked from home and rarely came into contact with others, even if they had already acquired the natural immunity many believed was superior in the first place. As it became increasingly clear these shots were, to put it mildly, not what they were cracked up to be—the reverse in fact—some, like their marketing exec Jaclyn Colbeth, had had enough. She fled her enviable media job in

New York and California to head south to what she, and others like her, thought would be freedom. She would run into some surprises of her own, as I will explain later. ∎

5

ROLLING OUT THE WRONG "WELCOME WAGON"

Others who left blue states behind, like realtor Dave Markowicz, were greatly concerned about schools promulgating so-called anti-racism and critical race theory and simultaneously informing children as early as kindergarten that their birth sex was only one of several options. These same kids were kept in masks, unable to see the facial expressions of their teachers and classmates, retarding their emotional development, not to mention their education, for years. This indoctrination continued into college and graduate school, with now even the most widely respected medical and law schools having "gone woke."

Dave and his wife Tally, parents of four, couldn't take any more of it. They and many other new internal migrants felt like second-class citizens in the land they loved and had had enough. They wanted to live in a place where freedom reigned. At least that's what they said was their motive. Others insisted that their move was financially motivated—that they wanted to live in a state with a cheaper standard of living and lower (or better yet no) state income taxes. Maybe it was a combination of these various factors. Those who wanted less government intrusion in their lives were also unlikely to want to cover in their taxes the costs of just these intrusions.

Many locals claimed that these blue staters were coming to their pristine red states not to join them, but to pollute them ideologically. Wittingly or unwittingly, migrants were carrying with them their liberal ideas and irreligious values. They were also bringing higher real estate prices that often pushed locals out of their homes and created traffic beyond anything their region was prepared for.

Some of these entrenched locals were admittedly cranks, but many are reasonable and prudent. These locals tended to appear regularly in the comments sections of right-leaning websites. Some even contemplated setting up "welcome wagons" for the blue staters to remind them of why they had come in the first place, and to gently remind them to check their virtue-signaling social justice bilge at the door.

I first saw this "welcome wagon" idea proffered years ago by University of Tennessee law professor Glenn Reynolds on his popular blog InstaPundit, though he has since reconsidered. Yet I thought he was 100 percent correct when he first, somewhat playfully, made the suggestion.

We were both wrong. The fear that blue staters were going to pollute red states with their indelible left-wing ideology, I came to learn, could not have been more baseless.

The problem, indeed, was just the opposite. ∎

6

THE RISE OF
A NEW CAVALRY

The newcomers were anything but liberal and progressive, overt or otherwise. They were American refugees: people who so rejected those ideologies, who so preferred to live in a constitutional republic, that they were willing to pull up stakes; quit their jobs; leave behind friends, family, and their accustomed ways of life; and trek across the country—all to live in accordance with their values.

Meanwhile, their destinations—the red states—had problems of their own. Most of them did, anyway.

Even reliably red Tennessee, which voted two-thirds for Donald Trump in 2020, had issues. Members of the Republican-dominated legislature were guilty or suspected of wire fraud and other assorted malfeasances. Yet more importantly, there was a significant disconnect between many of the legislators and their voters. A list of desires from the state's conservative citizenry, for everything from educational reform to election integrity, went unanswered. In the worst cases, politicians reneged on their promises, betraying their constituents. Tennessee was, with some exceptions, entrenched in a corruption similar to that which crept into and then nearly dominated many red-leaning and swing states, Georgia being a salient example. In Tennessee, the corruption was better hidden.

Some likened the incumbent Republicans governing those states, very much including Tennessee, to the old Southern Democrats—a good ol' boys' (and these days good ol' girls') club. They were not exactly wolves in sheep's clothes, but rather animals of their own kind, spouting "conservative" rhetoric replete with promises they would rarely fulfill and in some cases never attempt to enact. It was business as usual, which really meant that business prevailed over the will of the people on issue after issue. Genuine conservative reform rarely got passed. From Arizona to South Carolina, you could call it "six degrees of RINOism."

So, when it came to welcome wagons, they were needed for an entirely unexpected reason: to help the arrivals, political refugees with their (sadly naive) patriotic and constitutional hopes and dreams, accustom themselves to disappointment with their new environment. To a number of those people, the reality on the ground was a considerable shock.

But out of this blow came a surprising opportunity. Many found themselves becoming the activists they had never been before, in some cases never thought of being, and in so doing discovered themselves. The red states were not the nirvana they sought, so they set out to make them one.

Perhaps the bravest and most effective of these activists I met was Kathleen Harms, a transplant with her husband, Tom, from Massachusetts. Despite having the most polite and mild-mannered affect, Kathy Harms was able to strike fear in the hearts of establishment politicians as she walked the halls of the Cordell Hull Building, where they had their offices.

Those newcomers were, in effect, a cavalry come to rescue the red states from themselves, to right (pun intended, if you wish) the ship. In their own way, they came straight out of a John Ford movie, now riding in on their SUVs to save their chosen states, to the constant encouragement of talk radio (first Rush Limbaugh and then, after his death, Clay Travis, Buck Sexton, and Glenn Beck) if not blaring bugles.

This rescue mission was bigger than the individual states. It involved the whole country in a sense that was both symbolic and practical, because hopes for a return to the constitutional republic envisioned by the Founders rested now, for better or worse, with the red states.

The blues had long since abandoned constitutional government in favor of a centralized and oppressive political system, one they desired to make even more autocratic in the wake of the pandemic. This hoped-for revolution had become known popularly as the "Great Reset." In essence this was a less overtly fascistic version of communist China, with pervasive political correctness, woke ideology, and cancel culture replacing forced organ transplants and internment camps, the levers of control used by the Chinese leadership. "You will own nothing, and you'll be happy" was the Great Reset's mantra via the World Economic Forum and its guru Klaus Schwab. This was a "bright, shining lie" designed to create a kind of high-tech feudalism where an entrenched rich class could remain in place, indeed gain further wealth and power, through mouthing social justice pieties.

Silicon Valley had already made that evolution easier, preparing the populace for a life of servitude to the state. Those companies had already built into their own systems an echo of the Chinese social credit score system which entails constant surveillance of the individual. In fact, some of them, early on, had instructed the Chinese on how to do it. For the citizen who wished to live free, to completely opt out and disconnect, this left John Galt's dream but an impractical solution in modern life. Few can do that.

That was only one of many problems complicating rescue by this ad hoc cavalry. It was fraught with multiple practical and psychological issues, some in place long before their arrival. Many good people, even a few good and honest politicians, already lived, and had for a long time, in the red states. They had a right to be offended, or at least a bit put off, by know-it-all newcomers trying to reinvent the wheel on issues they had been struggling with for years. And the cavalry itself was not always pure. Saboteurs existed in its ranks, as were some who got ahead of themselves—who were "out over their skis," as the saying goes—not to mention others who were simply inept.

The task facing us refugees was daunting. In the four-plus years I have been in Tennessee, the world as we knew it has fallen apart. We've seen the arrival of the pandemic; the still-contested election of Joe Biden; the immediate reversal of Donald Trump's policies, notably on energy; ever-increasing violence in our city streets with an escalating murder rate, largely among minorities; riots in Portland and Seattle; the burning of government buildings by Antifa and Black Lives Matter (BLM); the events of January 6, 2021, laced with FBI subterfuge; rampant inflation with supply chain failures; the debacle in Afghanistan; and the Ukraine war, to name just a few remarkable developments.

And now, at the end of this book's editing process and having just passed the five-year mark in my Tennessee residency, I and everyone else are faced with the unprecedented indictment of the forty-fifth president of the United States and Republican favorite in the coming election by the clearly weaponized Justice Department of the opposite party. Where this will lead is unknowable.

The republic is being tested as it has never been since World War II. It seems almost as if the nation is about to fly apart, either by states seceding or even by a second civil war. Such things are being talked about for the first time in decades—perhaps not widely, but enough to enter the public mind. Thomas Jefferson's ominous comment to William Smith—"God forbid we should ever be 20 years without such a rebellion [as the American Revolution]"—is resurfacing in the public conversation.

A more pragmatic quote that keeps popping up is former Speaker of the House Tip O'Neill's "all politics is local"—and for good reason. The realm of politics that the people could change was mostly local, indeed almost entirely local. Whether or not the refugee cavalry were aware of O'Neill's quote, his principle was motivating their actions and continues to do so. The battle to retrieve America is being fought in the local sphere, because here is the best place for it to be fought by the ordinary citizen. ∎

7

PUTTING ON MY FEDORA

I joined in my own way, at first as an observer, writing for the *Epoch Times*, but gradually and probably inevitably as a participant, though a hidden one, since I was trying to hold onto my journalistic independence and "impartiality," as if such things existed.

Part of what prompted me to take part was the same curiosity that had inspired me years before to become a detective novelist, as I had been for a time. It was a desire to explore—really to understand, if that were possible—the mysterious world behind the curtain.

And the South certainly has one. It abounds in mystery. The twists and turns of the events that transpired and continue to transpire during the struggle to keep the state of Tennessee red, honestly red, could fill a wall of suspense novels. Unwinding those events might tell us as much about the state of our politics and institutions, locally and nationally, as any lecture or academic essay could. Call it the human factor, always getting in the way of rational analysis.

For instance, why exactly did a man who ran Nashville's and Tennessee's most prominent and well-attended monthly power luncheon for conservatives wind up dead at the bottom of his stairs, with no explanation other than "he fell"? Was Tim Skow a secret drinker, drowning his loneliness and divorce in booze, to a degree that he couldn't stand up?

Talk was that he had been saying "strange things" in the days before his death. What did that mean? What things? Why was no autopsy performed? Skow was one of the first people I met after moving to the city. He had invited me for drinks for reasons I wasn't able to ascertain at the time and still have not.

His death occurred but weeks after Donald J. Trump, out of nowhere, endorsed a young woman for the newly gerrymandered—excuse me, redistricted—Tennessee Fifth Congressional District. Morgan Ortagus, celebrity Fox News contributor from Washington DC and former spokeswoman (spox, in the parlance) for a secretary of state, no less, had moved to Tennessee only two months before. Her candidacy led to accusations of carpetbagging from local conservatives, some of whom, you may not be surprised to hear, wanted the coveted congressional seat for themselves or their friends.

Before that, another relative carpetbagger who announced for the Fifth, this one from Southern California with then maybe two years in Nashville (the exact number is under dispute), got caught lying about his voting record on the same radio show where I regularly appeared, the *Tennessee Star Report*. (He claimed he had voted in Republican primaries—a requirement for running—but hadn't.) A music video director, Robby Starbuck had been until then remarkably popular with us refugees for his outspoken views on educational bias and election reform. Charismatic in an almost cultish way—he was a kind of modern-day Elmer Gantry, though in his early thirties, dressed in black, and sporting a ponytail— Starbuck remained popular and enjoyed the near-blind devotion of some of his followers. So what if he lied? They all do it anyway, after all. He was their guy.

This meant also ignoring photos that started to appear on the internet of his goth nuptials, the happy couple dressed like extras in the *Addams Family*, with a wedding cake constructed of skulls—only the event theme wasn't supposed to be funny. His wife, apparently, had at one time recorded songs as something resembling a satanist witch; whether sincerely or as an act was undetermined. Then people learned that Starbuck had made a gangsta rap video for a song titled "Enormous," in which a leading rapper endlessly touts the size of his member. Others said he had worked in the California porn industry as an editor, a rumor that has never been confirmed. Nevertheless, the music video was made barely more than a year before he was standing in front of audiences of Tennessee parents assuring them that, if elected, he would protect their children from the evils of critical race theory, not to mention the nauseating "grooming" and early-childhood gender obsession sweeping the nation's schools. ■

8

ARRIVEDERCI, STARBUCK
E ORTAGUS

Both of these people—the Washington insider Morgan Ortagus and the video director Robby Starbuck—were struck from the ballot in late April 2022 by the Tennessee Republican Party's State Executive Committee (SEC), a group of elected volunteers described to me as the type of people who "stood out in the rain for the party." This was perhaps an exaggeration, but not an excessive one. These loyalists had rejected the appeal of the two outsiders by an overwhelming vote, 13–3.

The consternation only grew. Trump had not been the sole national figure weighing in on the humble Tennessee Fifth. Actually, there had been a baker's dozen or more. None other than Senator Rand Paul of Kentucky had been fundraising for the videographer, while the highly regarded former ambassador to Germany and sometime director of national intelligence Richard Grenell had first adamantly backed one candidate and then the other, as if nobody would notice the switch.

Immediately after the SEC vote, South Carolina's Senator Lindsey Graham launched a scurrilous Twitter attack on the committee members, ugly and beyond reason, without evincing the slightest knowledge of what happened, why it happened, or who they were. All he knew was that he didn't like them. They were deep staters in disguise (he should know), and he insisted their behavior should nullify Nashville's attempt to be the location of the 2024 GOP National Convention. The city was known to be in competition then with Milwaukee for the lucrative event. Despite its obvious superiority to Milwaukee as a convention site (the city is nicknamed "NashVegas" for a reason), Nashville lost out on the opportunity due to chicanery by its Democratic mayor John Cooper and its Metro Council, plus incompetence by the Republican National Committee.

I ended up being involved myself, writing a column for the *Epoch Times* that earned the eternal opprobrium of Robby Starbuck. His anger was expressed to me directly in hostile text messages and indirectly on Twitter, even though I had absented myself from that social media company long before it became notorious for censoring the Hunter Biden laptop story. By the time this all happened, I was being referred to on that same radio show as "Old Hickory"—in honor of local hero President Andrew Jackson, whom I didn't resemble in any way, shape, or form—because I was approaching four years in Nashville, far longer than the would-be congressional candidates. It was a joke, of course. (In December 2022, I attempted via text message to reconnect with Starbuck to get his side of the story for this book, but I was met with silence.) ∎

9

CLANDESTINE CONNECTIONS

Michael Patrick Leahy was host of the *Tennessee Star Report*, a right-leaning political talk show that ran from five to eight every weekday morning. (I never made it on before seven.) Once a leader of the Tea Party movement, Leahy had founded, with talk show host Steve Gill, the Star Network, an alliance of similar radio programs and news websites across the South and lately into Pennsylvania, Iowa, Georgia, and Michigan. Leahy liked to start my segments by announcing that I had once been his boss. I had. But that was long ago, back in Los Angeles, when I was running PJ Media and PJTV. I was a neophyte in the South compared to most of his guests—well, except for those two nationally hailed congressional candidates.

I learned much about Tennessee politics from Leahy, but I learned some of the juicer parts of what I have written about the congressional race from that shadowy figure I mentioned earlier, found online at a website called Sons of Rocky Top. "Rocky Top," a bluegrass hit first recorded by the Osborne Brothers in the sixties, and many times by others thereafter, was one of Tennessee's state songs.

It turned out, however, that this particular "Son" of Rocky Top, as I came to realize on our secret hour-long phone calls, was no local yokel or dime-a-dozen gossip. He knew where most of the bodies were buried in Tennessee government, from the governor down, but he also had spent about twenty-five years in Washington, DC, working at the very top of the Republican Party, sometimes at the presidential level. He was connected, and then some. But his identity was a deeply buried mystery, so much so that he told me if he identified himself to his colleagues as the perpetrator of this scandalous blog, they would be astonished, even flabbergasted.

Rocky had his theories about what would happen in the congressional race, given that the two carpetbaggers had received, in his eyes, their just desserts. He thought that Starbuck's shrill threats to sue unless allowed to run were hollow, and that Ortagus would ultimately avail herself, with her husband and young child, of the one-way Nashville-to-DC Southwest Airlines schedule Rocky Top had cheekily posted for her benefit online.

I wasn't so sure.

Meanwhile, a third newcomer, this one a former pastor and later microbrewery owner from Texas, had almost simultaneously formed a statewide organization to take on the powers that be in the Tennessee legislature that he claimed worked against the interest of the Republican rank-and-file. (He had a point, but was that enough?) Gary Humble has gone so far as to run for office against the Speaker of the Senate, Jack Johnson, a man some called the most powerful in the state (after the governor) and who affected the style of a good ol' boy to a T (he led his own country band that was actually pretty good) while, according to some, double-dealing behind the voters' backs. Most recently Johnson had reneged on a public promise to get rid of suspicious voting machines and replace them with paper ballots.

Also, almost at the same time, one of the most celebrated new conservative internet media companies moved into Metro Nashville amid fanfare they were going to bypass Hollywood, start producing films and television, and move the culture to the right.

They were to be followed, only a year or two later, by an actual Hollywood television and movie star, equally well known for his support of veterans, who moved his base of operations from Los Angeles to nearby Franklin. These were only the latest examples of the area being trumpeted as the new home of a burgeoning right-wing intelligentsia both creative and theoretical, the problem being that many of them, following the grand tradition of Freud's "narcissism of small differences," barely tolerated each other and rarely talked.

On the face of it, it did not appear that any of these seemingly disparate events and trends were necessarily connected. Nevertheless, I intended to look into them and several others of their ilk in order to make the proverbial heads and tails out of them. Whatever emerged, I am convinced that the sixties radicals were right when they said that the personal is political. They were also right when they said that you were either part of the solution or part of the problem.

I always thought these radicals just got the political sides flipped—and they certainly did. Huey Newton and company were themselves part of the problem in extremis. Both sides, however, are more complicated than I had assumed. My move to Tennessee taught me that.

So if you find me using some of the cheapjack tricks of the mystery writer, please excuse me. I know they do not traditionally appear in serious books of political or social analysis, and I am not employing them just to make you turn the page, though that wouldn't hurt.

I am not attempting to write one of those traditional political or social books anyway. It is my contention that such analyses, without acknowledgment of the private behaviors and needs of those involved, present only a partial, and often misleading, version of what transpired—just some of the truth and not always the most important part.

Further, I realize on a subtextual level that I will be treading where my betters, to say the least—people like Winston Churchill and E. M. Forster—have already planted their estimable poles, questioning the limits of democracy as it's practiced, asking whether it is merely the best of several imperfect systems, or trying to define just how many cheers it deserves: one, two, or three. Tennessee, it turned out for me, was a petri dish for such an investigation.

As most of us know, although sometimes we forget or suppress, the people who wheel and deal to make the proverbial sausage of our laws, and those who make executive decisions, almost always have more on their minds than the efficacy of those decisions. More often than not, what is at play in our politics is not Left and Right, Republican and Democrat, or even socialist and capitalist, but the familiar human litany of pride, greed, envy, sloth, and lust, resulting in what John Dalberg-Acton, a.k.a. Lord Acton, long ago told us of power—that it "tends to corrupt, and absolute power corrupts absolutely."

Less known, and yet more ominous, was what he further said in that same oft-quoted letter to an Anglican bishop: "Great men are almost always bad men."

That is what the cavalry was up against. ■

10

MEET "THE CAVALRY"

"What is it about you Californians?," Galen Walker recounted the man asking him disdainfully.

We were sitting in the patio of Galen and his wife Kathy's Bold Patriot Brewing Company, which they moved from Norco, California, to Nashville, Tennessee, in 2019. The man in question was state senator Jack Johnson, a major player in the Tennessee General Assembly and a kingpin of the Republican establishment.

The two men had been arguing, rather vociferously apparently, about COVID restrictions, lockdowns, masks, and such. It could have been vaccine mandates. Galen didn't remember the precise topic when I talked with him, but it was clear they were on opposite sides. Galen—a tall fellow in his seventies with graying whiskers that make him look like a Civil War general—had been adamantly on the side of medical freedom (ergo, no mandated shots), and claimed masks were a "fashion statement," as talk show host Clay Travis wittily deemed them. A libertarian sort, Galen had had those views long before he moved to Tennessee.

Johnson and Galen had started as friends. Senator Jack Johnson was a respected conservative, Tennessee-style, and aside from his political career, he was a pretty good semi-pro country guitarist and singer who played with a band called the Austin

Brothers. Galen had heard them and twice invited them to play at his brewery.

I had seen Johnson's band on a couple of occasions myself and, after having heard Bill Clinton mangle the saxophone, was impressed that any politician could play halfway decently. If I had to rate Johnson's abilities on the guitar, I would say he was several notches above former Arkansas governor Mike Huckabee.

But music isn't politics, and I assumed the senator was a typical conservative red-state politician when, only a couple of months after my arrival in Music City, we found ourselves sitting side by side at neighboring microphones on Michael Patrick Leahy's *Tennessee Star Report* morning radio show, both of us bloviating on the issues du jour.

What naivete. I didn't realize then what a typical conservative red-state politician might be, how broad and variable that classification actually was—or why they (some of them at least) might be so irritated with incoming Californians.

Galen Walker and Jack Johnson had a lot to disagree about besides healthcare, such as the use of voting machines. It was the refugee from California, ironically, who was taking the more staunchly conservative position on election integrity.

As for Johnson, after the outcry of fraud following the 2020 election, at first he indicated he opposed the machine's use in his Williamson County polling places, but little changed. Voting machines stayed put. I suspect he believed deep down that too much money had already been spent on them, too many relationships established with vendors and lobbyists, to get rid of them now. Paper ballots cost next to nothing. They weren't good for business, and the business of America, to paraphrase Calvin Coolidge, is business. Besides, the machines really worked. No one had proved otherwise, unless you believed that nutcase who sold pillows.

Or did they?

Galen was pretty sure voting machines were high-tech booby-traps inviting software sabotage. For Johnson's part, he probably thought, What do these ungrateful people want, to go back to Santa Monica and have some social justice warrior spray-paint "white supremacist" on their garage door or, worse yet, leave feces in their mailbox? Tennessee was a Southern Democrat bastion not so long ago. Who do you think changed that? Who made it the second-lowest tax state in the nation, with a deficit-free treasury second to none?

He also had a point.

I wanted to ask another local his opinion about the motivation of the newcomers—especially one with sufficiently diverse knowledge of the state and the people coming into it—so I spoke with Brandon Lewis, who founded the Tennessee Conservative website in late 2020, just when the pandemic was beginning to dominate the national psyche. Lewis is a true Southerner, born in Alabama of Cherokee stock and now a resident of the Chattanooga area.

Lewis's website took off rapidly, and soon he was getting subscribers and emails not just from within the state but as many as 7 percent, he estimates, from across the country. He believes the 2020 pandemic was the primary motivating event for the surge in migrants (whom I call the refugees), but he also believes Donald Trump was a strong inspiration. Trump was able to, as he put it, "discredit the media to the point where people for the first time felt like, hey, what I am seeing is a bunch of BS.... I think Donald Trump gave people permission to have a backbone."

Fifty percent of the people who now write for Lewis's Tennessee Conservative are transplants, he said. He also added, vis-à-vis the mission of his site, "If what people here are trying to do...the ones you call the refugees and others...get their efforts screwed over by those media lackeys, where the heck do you go?"

Where indeed?

My discussions with Galen Walker and Brandon Lewis occurred before the 2022 election, when Jack Johnson, undoubtedly to his astonishment, would find himself almost losing his coveted slot as the state senator from Williamson County—one of the wealthiest Republican counties in the nation—to the aforementioned Gary Humble, a virtually unknown migrant from Texas who was himself backed by many of the California transplants Johnson so reviled.

The question was whether that near upset, with the incumbent winning by only slightly more than seven hundred votes, was a harbinger of great change to come in the state. The newcomers were already making an impact. Few people were more of a local institution than Senator Jack Johnson.

And that electoral surprise occurred in supposedly red Williamson County, not blue Davidson County, contiguous with Nashville. One thing my wife and I shared with Galen and Kathy Walker is that when we moved hearth and home from California, none of us realized Nashville was blue nor, if we had an inkling, took it seriously. It couldn't really be *blue* blue. Not blue like the woke-opolises of LA and San Francisco. And it wasn't, of course, but it was bluer than we had imagined. We had thought Tennessee red, ergo Nashville red, or at least purple.

It was naive of all of us. Big cities all over the red states are hotbeds of a reactionary and self-destructive form of liberalism that seeks to turn those states blue from the cities outward, with carless populaces stacked in high-rise buildings, moving about only on public transport and, when possible, working in cubbies like characters in a dystopian novel or film. The wide-open spaces would be open no more. Who would grow the food would be a mystery, unless it was Microsoft billionaire Bill Gates who was evidently buying much of the world's arable land along with communist China.

As I would find out, Nashville and Tennessee would be a test case in this depressing process whose conclusion is nowhere near resolved.

Indeed, the Walkers themselves ended up in Nashville, if not by default, then somewhat by accident. The original Bold Patriot Brewery was successful in Norco, in an area of Southern California known as the Inland Empire that was relatively conservative, at least until recently. As they did later in Nashville, Galen taught Revolutionary War history there to patrons, in part from a Hillsdale College syllabus. The problem was the venue was too small to make a profit.

After a difficult search, they found a new larger location that would work, but it had a caveat. They had to sign a ten-year lease. When Galen asked his partners whether they could see themselves living in California in ten years, to a man and woman they instantly said no. That was that.

When Galen secured the venue for his Nashville brewery in a gentrifying shopping mall off Charlotte Avenue, before he even moved in an irate woman circulated an email to the dozen or so other tenants to beware, that a "racist" was coming to their mall. Welcome to Tennessee!

That wasn't to say Nashville wasn't miles better than LA, New York, or Chicago. It was, but if he had known better, Galen thinks now, he would have moved to neighboring Williamson County, which was more red.

From what I gathered, Senator Johnson and Galen more or less buried the hatchet at the end of their argument, but that was only a temporary hiatus in an ongoing struggle. The migration occurring from blue states to red had unintended consequences, and it caused unforeseen conflicts that teetered on the edge of exploding. ■

11

WHERE CAVALRY ARE BILLETED

Westhaven is a housing development a few miles west of downtown Franklin, which is itself twenty-two miles south of Nashville and sometimes considered a suburb and sometimes a burgeoning small city of its own. These days it's more often referred to as the latter.

The development in many ways resembles a mega-cute Disney community in the style of the original Disneyland before it went woke and started talking about putting "canonical trans characters" on its theme park rides, only to be pushed back by Florida governor Ron DeSantis.

Originally a liberal redoubt, Westhaven had become a magnet for conservative newcomers—from California, New York, and Illinois especially. This although Olivia Shupe, one of those migrants, told me the construction was on the shoddy side. After she and her husband Jeff had rented one of the cute cheek-by-jowl homes, they were about to take the plunge and buy one.

Her husband agreed. He was in that business and knew. They were buying for the community, the neighbors, not the construction. And the development had a great clubhouse with an ample meeting room for activists like them to do their thing. Recently, I learned a wealthy conservative couple moved from what might be the toniest neighborhood in Nashville—Northumberland, a gated community where the city's most glamorous couple, Oscar-winning actress Nicole Kidman and multiple Grammy–winning singer Keith Urban, live—to Westhaven to be part of their activist community.

Anyway, you could have fooled me about the construction there. Everything looked so neat and tidy you expected "It's a Small World" to be blasting from speakers while kids cavorted in the fields with their golden retrievers and Frisbees.

Indeed, this was precisely what inspired the Shupes—refugees most recently, after having lived around the world, from Redding, a relative whistlestop on California's 5 Freeway—to pull over in their car when they saw this Norman Rockwell–like scene. They never left. Jeff indeed upped the construction ante by forming Patriot Pools.

Nearby Franklin itself was like a larger, modern version of a Rockwell painting, a picture-perfect downtown as if copied from a fraying *Saturday Evening Post* cover, but with sushi bars and designer ice cream added, not to mention trendy clothing stores with names like the Barn Door Co. This was the place to go if you wanted to pick up the most recherché items, Southern-style. At the almost too precious for words Leiper's Fork—an unincorporated village close to Franklin and Westhaven and part of the same basic neighborhood—you could uncover the likes of a 1944 D-28 Martin guitar or even a 1963 Everly Brothers model at the Pickin' Corner.

This would all seem, at first glance, to be merely capitalizing on nostalgia for an America that many felt, with unfortunate justification, was vanishing. But slightly beneath the surface it was also based on a fervent desire to preserve what was left, even to bring back what had gone.

That was not so much the strike-it-rich American Dream, but one of freedom, God, and family, in whatever order you choose. This was a natural part of pursuing the life, liberty, and happiness that was demanded by the Founders in their Declaration of

Independence. To do this in Franklin and environs was especially attractive because it was the seat of Williamson County, among the more affluent Republican counties in the USA—and according to some, at one point the most affluent. Couched in bucolic rolling hills, it has attracted luminaries like talk show host Clay Travis, Senator Marsha Blackburn, and country singer/songwriter and *American Idol* host Luke Bryan, to move in. Some country stars even bring with them with their personal herds of Black Angus. Other residents enjoy a more conventional lifestyle, but one that would still be the envy of 99 percent of humanity.

This included people who would normally be classified somewhere on that ever-sliding scale of the middle class. Many of the cavalry, like the Shupes, were among them. Their price to pay, they originally assumed, would be, as the population inevitably increased, at worst an increasingly onerous commute to Nashville, should they work there. Employment opportunities in Music City abounded, if not in the highly competitive music industry itself, then in the business that had actually made Metro Nashville wealthy—healthcare. The city is home to the Hospital Corporation of America, which operates 186 hospitals and approximately two thousand sites of care in twenty-one states and the United Kingdom as of 2020.

Of course, with so many people working at home, and businesses of all sorts expanding into the suburban Franklin area (including next-door Brentwood, whose place in the community ironically, although not quite as lavishly, mirrored Brentwood, California, in West Los Angeles), the increasingly difficult commute was diminishing in importance. People were moving in droves to Williamson County because they could have their proverbial cake and eat it too: a great environment; seemingly freedom-loving and patriotic; and, most important, reputedly some of the best public schools in the state, if not in the entire country, to educate their children.

Those same schools, however, turned out to be the inkblot staining the Rockwell painting. Something was wrong. Very wrong, as it turned out. ∎

12

ENTER THE FIRST MARKOWICZ

Dave Markowicz, a real estate agent formerly from Santa Monica, was explaining all this to me over the latte-of-the-day in one of those cute little coffee shops that proliferate in places like Franklin. Such establishments demonstrated the degree to which blue and red states had already blended—culturally, if not politically—in the more upscale areas. Markowicz, fed up with California for reasons similar to mine, was another member of the cavalry, but in a different manner from the Shupes. More businessman than activist—although later I noticed him, almost inevitably, becoming a strong one—he had moved with his family two years before and opened a realty office in Franklin. Presciently, however, he had not closed his office in Santa Monica. His company could then sell people's California houses while helping them find new digs in Williamson. Business was booming beyond his expectations, but he had certain regrets. You might even call it guilt. He had used the schools as part of the allure to his fellow Californians but now, via his own children and stories he was hearing, realized those same schools were part of the problem—the major part, actually—and not the solution. The conflict it was creating for him was driving him toward activism.

If Williamson County could not be the true American nirvana, what could be? Was that real American Dream possible, not the kind criticized or satirized by left-wing novelists but something less self-serving and closer to civic decency? That seemed attainable back in 1835, when Alexis de Tocqueville—despite his often-accurate criticisms, particularly of the mediocre level of our politicians—praised the nation in his *Democracy in America*. Why shouldn't it be attainable now? More and more disillusioned newcomers like Markowicz were becoming activists.

The Shupes, though, were activists from way back, already having made their local school board uncomfortable in Redding, so much so that they themselves were feeling uncomfortable in their hometown. The family—they had four children already in early adulthood—sought greener pastures, only to discover that there were a lot of weeds growing in their new, supposedly pristine fields. The same progressive cant was being taught in the Tennessee schools. In fact, it was in many ways worse in Tennessee, emerging out of an educational curriculum euphemistically titled Wit & Wisdom that aimed to inculcate progressive values in school children from kindergarten onward. These included masqueraded versions of critical race theory and what was obviously inappropriate sexual education for very young children. A battle was being waged by local parents. ∎

13

FIRST FIX THE SCHOOLS

Olivia Shupe joined the fight, becoming the person who directed the vetting of those who wanted to run for school board and county commissioner positions under the banner of the newly formed group, Williamson Families. A similar battle in Loudon County, Virginia, had gripped the country, inspiring the organizing in Williamson, where, it seemed on the surface, the struggle would be an easier one. Williamson Families had been formed by Robin Steenman, a former bomber pilot who reached the rank of major in Afghanistan. Steenman wasn't the only veteran in the group. Franklin and its vicinity were filled with retired military upset with the direction their country had taken, many of whom were at the forefront of local organizing. But it was Steenman who seized the moment of parental discontent and fashioned a functioning organization, first under the banner of a local chapter of the existing Moms for Liberty. Steenman was then working in conjunction with Lori Friedheim, a Filipina American UC Berkeley graduate in the sciences who functioned as their director of research.

At first things were going well, with a large crowd appearing for an educational meeting at a Harley-Davidson dealership, a venue that had "Southern conservative" written all over it and also provided a certain macho charisma. Nearly everyone stopped to admire the bikes. The event occurred under a tent erected behind the dealership that was filled to the brim with agitated parents. There Steenman and others informed their audience, many of whom were new refugees brought from other states by the supposedly stellar public schools, at length about the dangers of the Wit & Wisdom curriculum that dominated those schools, at least from kindergarten through eighth grade, with the potential to do more.

Attendees learned of Wit & Wisdom's fascination, really obsession, with race. Second graders had a nine-week module titled "Civil Rights Heroes," with two particularly controversial books: *Ruby Bridges Goes to School: My True Story* by Ruby Bridges and *The Story of Ruby Bridges* by Robert Coles. Both featured illustrations of white children viciously taunting the black Ruby on her way to integrate a school back in the civil rights era, the implication being that things hadn't really changed. It was the same today, or so the curriculum said: whites suppress blacks and blacks are oppressed from birth. Was this good for children in any way?

Critical race theory and its yet more insidious brother, "antiracism," were hidden not so far beneath the surface of this module. For the adherents of this approach, a person's fate is determined by the individual's race or sex, not by the content of his or her character, as was famously envisioned by Dr. Martin Luther King. Almost every moral person, most of us thought, agreed with the color-blind approach, and had for a long time. But the goal posts had been moved, the crowd at Harley-Davidson was learning—not just by Antifa and Black Lives Matter demonstrations-cum-riots in Seattle and Portland, but in their children's classrooms right there in the Republican heartland of Williamson County. A kind of covert radicalism was being taught under the meretricious mantle of social justice.

Wit & Wisdom—a product of Great Minds, formerly Common Core, Inc., which had given us something called "holistic" Eureka Math, speaking of opaque rhetoric—also came under fire for inappropriately presenting sexual materials to children not yet mature enough to handle them. Not far behind was the concept of "grooming," the encouragement of young children to explore or even adopt alternative gender identities before they were able to read and write with anything approaching fluency. Chemical "puberty blockers" were at hand, ready to aid in this bizarre and premature transition from which there was, most likely, no return. No one knew anywhere near the full scientific implications of this process, how it would affect the patients over the course of their lives—physically, emotionally, or intellectually. Parents were loudly wondering, How could such things be taught or recommended in conservative Tennessee? How could we have packed up our belongings and crossed the country for this?

Williamson Families stood against it all, although some of their more extreme accusations were denied by Williamson School authorities. Steenman wrote an extensive letter to Tennessee Education Commissioner Dr. Penny Schwinn. Berkeley-grad Schwinn was herself a subject of controversy, not only because she was an unlikely choice for the position by a supposedly conservative governor—rumors flew that Bill Gates had something to do with her selection—but also because of conflict-of-interest accusations: her husband worked for a company that had an $8 million contract with the Tennessee Department of Education, signed by Penny Schwinn herself. (Schwinn has recently resigned and was replaced by Lizette Gonzalez Reynolds, whom, we are told by Governor Lee's office, has a career that "reflects a deep commitment to school choice, assessment, and accountability." Local critics were saying this was the proverbial distinction without a difference.) An excerpt of Steenman's letter to Schwinn regarding Wit & Wisdom reads as follows:

> The narrow and slanted obsession on historical mistakes reveals a
> heavily biased agenda, one that makes children hate their country,
> each other, and/or themselves. This outcome has been proven

with multiple testimonies of the negative change in behavior or outlook by their children. The relentless nature of how these divisive stories is taught (*sic*), the lack of historical context and difference in perspective, and the manipulative pedagogy all work together to amplify and sow feelings of resentment, shame of one's skin color, and/or fear.

This was all true enough. But the extensive letter seems to have made little impact on the education commissioner. Later it was discovered that at least some Williamson children were learning to read via "The GAYBCs"—B is for Bi, C is for Coming Out, D is for Drag, T is for Trans, and so forth. This caused such a parental uproar, however, that the local education authorities were forced to react. "The GAYBCs" were removed from the iPads the children took home with them for homework. The presence of this educational method in the first place, those same authorities now insisted, had been an oversight.

Steenman, Shupe, and other activists in their group, largely refugees, followed up the Harley-Davidson event with a much bigger gathering at the Factory—one of those formerly industrial spaces gussied up with boutiques and food halls, this one including a meeting space that could accommodate a significant crowd with a balcony and a VIP section attached. By this point Steenman's group had left the Mothers for Liberty and formed a political action committee, "Williamson Families PAC," to facilitate the raising and dispensation of money. Their name was inspired by the Southlake Families PAC of Southlake, Texas, which had had success battling an old guard chamber of commerce and electing school board members who favored a more classical education. This name and organizational change on the part of the Williamson Families was ostensibly meant to encourage men to join the fight too, to make it a family affair, but also because of political in-fighting within the Mothers for Liberty organization. ■

14

MONTY PYTHON COMES TO TENNESSEE

This obsession with nomenclature common to political groups was satirized brilliantly and hilariously in Monty Python's *Life of Brian* (1979), a comedic film set in the biblical era. An "aghast" John Cleese informs an innocent fruit seller who has misidentified his cadre of conspirators, "The Judean People's Front?!... We're the People's Front of Judea!" The scene is a classic. It represents an attitude at the polar opposite of Ronald Reagan's admonition, "No enemies on the right," though few on the right seem to be heeding Reagan's wisdom today.

In the case of the Williamson Families, people began to mutter that Steenman, a transplant from Texas, was making the movement too much about her. She was the one who made all the statements and gave all the interviews. She was the one taking the meetings with authorities, with Tennessee governor Bill Lee, and with his heavily criticized education commissioner Schwinn. Shouldn't they have gone as a small group with legal help in tow when dealing with professional politicians? Wasn't there safety—and power—in numbers?

Nevertheless, despite whatever splits had already occurred and whatever grumbling was going on behind the scenes, the

Williamson Families managed to bring together a sizable crowd at the Factory. Part of the attraction was the advertised presence of country star John Rich, one of the more publicly committed conservatives among the many famous local musicians, if not the most—with the possible exception of the irrepressible Kid Rock. Rock (né Robert James Ritchie) is himself a transplant from Michigan now ensconced in Metro Nashville, with his own multistory nightclub on Lower Broadway not far from Rich's. He would soon be recording his ultra-MAGA anthem "We the People" standing in front of the flag as he rapped lyrics telling the establishment to go you-know-where with every expletive he could muster. It worked well, at least from my point of view. Later, he logged in on the Budweiser/trans controversy by blowing some beer cans to smithereens with what looked like an AK-47.

Others were said to be MAGA-sympathetic but remained closeted. There were vocal exceptions, including, notably, Brittany Aldean, the wife of country musician Jason, who regularly broadcast her right-wing views via Twitter. Soon enough her megastar husband was following suit.

Rich himself had appeared frequently on the Fox Network in support of conservative causes. Lately he had become a backer of something called the Old Glory Bank, a financial institution in Oklahoma being repurposed to keep money safe from government control as digital currency became more widely used. He also gave fundraisers at his palatial, skyline-view Nashville home replete with a guitar-shaped swimming pool, a bandstand to rival most nightclubs, and an enormous elevator lined with photos of Rich with every country luminary from Johnny Cash to Aldean, for whom he wrote smash hit songs. I attended one of these fundraisers for Senator Marsha Blackburn's 2018 campaign—John and others played for hours. It was definitely an only-in-Nashville event and one of the few political fundraisers worth the steep price of admission for the entertainment alone.

The gathering at the Factory, however, was less successful, although well attended. Putatively organized to introduce candidates for the school board and other county positions, the meeting began with a lengthy speech by Steenman, which was followed by similarly long speeches from Jeremy Slayden, a retired baseball player, and Leigh-Allyn Baker, an actress who starred in a Disney Channel sitcom in the 2010s. The latter two apparently had been drafted to bring in the crowds, but, unlike Rich, they were far from A-list stars. One wondered if they brought in anyone other than their neighbors and a couple of relatives. The people were impatient during their speeches. They had come to hear from the nominees, especially for school board, a position that had recently risen in importance to the equivalent of senator for conservative activists and naturally for the refugees, some of whom would themselves run for office. Unfortunately, due to the length of the "celebrity" appearances, much of the audience left before the candidates were given a brief window to introduce themselves.

As a member of the press, I had met a few of these candidates before the event in a balcony area cordoned off for interviews. Paradoxically and almost uniformly, those with the least formal contact with education as a profession seemed to better understand the extreme ideological bias that had taken over our school systems at all levels. I realized, after only a few questions, that most of those with education degrees had already been effectively hypnotized and were victims of what has been called "mass formation psychosis," in the terminology of the Belgian academic Mattias Desmet. I wondered at the time why the Williamson Families had selected them. Fortunately, there were only few of that type; as I was told months afterward, they had slipped through the process because the group wished to have a full slate of candidates. Many of the best candidates, in my judgment, were newcomers, or relatively so, to the state. It was unclear, however, if any of them would prevail. Other than Steenman, who was not running and believed herself more useful as an organizer, they didn't appear to have a leader or even a flag-bearer competing for the school board to draw attention to the cause.

Shortly after this event, I received via email what was apparently a clandestine video of the establishment Williamson County Republican Party officials, coaching their would-be candidates for school board. These were the potential adversaries of the Williamson Families nominees. As if prepped to do so, one of those conventional party aspirants blurted out his concern that he had not voted in any Republican primaries, it normally being a requirement to have voted in at least three recent ones in order to run. He was assured immediately by an official not to worry, that there were "workarounds," that everything was possible with a donation of "time or money."

Watching that video—set in the generic meeting room of a chain hotel or community center that could have been anywhere in America—I thought I was staring into the dark underbelly of our politics, a small-time version of Boss Tweed at Tammany Hall. Was democracy even possible if, in the tiniest of elections, it was reduced to some sort of low-rent corrupt game orchestrated by the local chamber of commerce? I wondered how much money was involved in something as seemingly routine as a school board nomination. It was the People's Front of Judea versus the Judean People's Front all over again, only worse. The establishment was masquerading as revolutionaries.

As it happened, for all the to-ing and fro-ing between the different groups and subgroups, only 11 percent of those eligible voted in the Williamson County Republican primary. Evidently, better organizing, better publicity, and, most of all, better, more charismatic leaders were needed to upset a self-satisfied establishment. Or so it seemed. ■

15

THE FIFTH CONGRESSIONAL DISTRICT GOES BIG-TIME

Anonymity was the opposite of the situation for the Republican nomination in the newly redistricted Tennessee Fifth Congressional District, where charisma dominated excessively and where two well-known newcomers—one self-made and the other Washington-made—were leading the pack for the nomination.

The self-made candidate was Robby Starbuck, né Robby Starbuck Newsom, the goth-styled video director I described earlier. He flaunted his Cuban-American background (on his mother's side) as a kind of anti-communist bona fide, though it was unclear what exactly his connection to Cuba was or if he could even speak decent Spanish. He arrived in the Nashville area sometime around 2019 (the exact date became a subject of debate). He, or others on his behalf, had bought a many-acre place in Leiper's Fork (whose title was also subject to later controversy) and within days was making a name for himself in the community. He seemed to be speaking everywhere. Starbuck—Did he drop the Newsom to avoid confusion with the California governor? He insists not—had considerable charisma and knew how to talk the talk, especially when it came to early childhood education. He was adamantly opposed to critical race theory and the heavy sexualizing of school curricula from kindergarten onward, issues that, as we have seen, had consumed Williamson County, his adopted home. He also supported electoral integrity and disagreed with the use of voting machines like the ones used in Tennessee—all good causes of the Right.

I was seduced by that charisma and was, at first, as much deceived by it as anyone. Getting wind of Robby near the end of 2020, I had lunch with him at a trendy restaurant in Franklin, the kind of place that acknowledges the provenance of its grits on the menu almost as if they were wines. I was immediately caught by his magnetic qualities, not to mention his hardcore conservative-libertarian views that comported with my belief that right-wingers were now the cool guys and leftists the square conformists. This guy had potential to be a winner and, like me, was from California. Much younger though he was, it was almost as if he would be my proxy. And like me, he had worked in the motion picture industry, somewhere anyway. (Take that, you "woke" morons of Burbank and West Hollywood.) Eager for a political scoop, I wrote one of the first articles about him for the *Epoch Times*, praising the new boy in town who was intending to run for Congress once the redistricting was clear. Robby and I became immediate text message buddies, and he even invited me to sit at his table at the overblown annual Tennessee Republican event known as the Statesmen's Dinner at the Music City Center, with House Minority Leader Kevin McCarthy as the keynote. Now, I am embarrassed to look back at that first article I wrote because it reads to a great degree like press agentry. To quote myself:

> Just the other day, *The Epoch Times* published a column of mine— "'The Deplorables' Must Cement Control of the Republican Party"—in which I wrote: "New leadership must be found and, in the tradition of Trump, we should be free to look outside the political class, just as our founders hoped." ... Little did I know ... well, to be honest, I kind of suspected it ... that the very

next day I would be sitting having lunch in the picture-perfect town of Franklin, Tennessee, with just such a person. Robby Starbuck is pretty close to a paradigm of what I think this new Republican candidate should be. He's young (31) and comes not from the conventional political world—yet another lawyer who did two years in the Beltway but now claims to abhor the Deep State, at least until the next job—but from the area that has been most shunned (stupidly) by Republicans…the culture. Robby Starbuck has been a very successful director and producer of music videos, working with groups like Metric, Natalie Portman, and The Smashing Pumpkins, the latter on the sound track of a well-received short he wrote and directed, as well as some rappers.

I called the short "well-received" pretty much on his say-so, because it more resembled a mediocre student film when I ultimately viewed it, with the usual lack of plot or story covered—hopefully but almost always unsuccessfully—by artsy symbolism. But I put aside my cinematographic quibbles. After all, Robby wasn't applying to be a member of the Motion Picture Academy; he was heading in a direction that at first glance was more societally useful—and yet I wondered.

Still, I socialized with him. For a while it seemed he and his wife, once a singer with a somewhat outré background, would appear at virtually every event we attended, large and small, almost by accident—or was it kismet? We joked about it. All the while, his local fame was growing. It almost seemed Robby had a lock on the Republican Fifth Congressional District nomination, and hence on a seat in Congress as one of its youngest members, along with Madison Cawthorn, with whom Robby later got into a controversial incident on the floor of Congress. He was collecting endorsements from national figures seemingly by the dozen, among them Senator Rand Paul, Representative Marjorie Taylor Greene, former Trump adviser and television personality Sebastian Gorka, and even former acting director of national intelligence Richard Grenell. Grenell was someone I had known for some time from California and greatly admired for his stint as ambassador to Germany, where he stood up to Angela Merkel on Iran and other issues. Robby had been endorsed by Grenell for a small-time Tennessee congressional race? That was impressive.

My wife and I showed up at Robby's official candidacy announcement party, which he held very early, before the boundaries of the new district were even declared. He averred that he would move to live actually *in* the district, once they were drawn, even though that wasn't required. It was also years before any election, and no one else had announced or even been rumored to run. This event was staged, for some reason, at an aging estate in East Nashville, sometimes known as the city's Brooklyn equivalent, replete with home recording studios and trendy ethnic restaurants mixed with ramshackle houses, but far away from any possible redistricted Fifth. The choice was odd and the attendees mostly white and young, the rappers and other black supporters promised by Robby notably absent. (I would learn later why he kept those worlds separate.) Both he and his wife gave speeches promising to heal that gaping hole everyone acknowledged between the public and conventional politicians. They seemed to be well received. His candidacy remained promising. ∎

16

CONSERVATIVE CHIC

Not much later, another event my wife and I attended, a cocktail party, was a peculiar mix of Tennessee with an intimate, supposedly chic affair you might have been invited to in Soho or Malibu, assuming you were on the proper list. It took place at the tonier Franklin digs of one of those Nashville songwriters who made fortunes in the music business but whose names wouldn't be recognized, since they rarely appeared in front of audiences. This man was clearly a conservative—although, like many in his business, a sub-rosa one—who kept a personal gun locker in his house approaching the size of a two-car garage, holding enough weapons (of every imaginable sort) to arm the defense force of a smaller African country. To call this songwriter merely a supporter of the Second Amendment would be an understatement of serious proportions. But we had been invited there not to admire his collection—though most of us did in fascination, having rarely seen anything this extensive in a private home; it was definitely the place to be if civil war broke out—but for what we were told was a small gathering of conservative media in the area. My friend Sean Davis of the Federalist was there, as were Robby and his wife (I guess his past as a video director made him a member of the media), as well as Ric Grenell, visiting the Nashville area and adding a certain DC panache to the gathering.

Also present was another brand-new arrival in Nashville: Morgan Ortagus, with her husband, the successful businessman Jonathan Weinberger. The two were married in May 2013 by none other than Supreme Court associate justice Ruth Bader Ginsburg. When I say "brand-new arrival," I mean that the Ortagus-Weinbergers had only moved to Music City days before. I didn't know at the small party that Ortagus would soon be dueling with Starbuck for the coveted nomination of the soon-to-be redistricted-as-pro-Republican Tennessee Fifth Congressional District. Perhaps Ortagus did, because shortly it would be announced that she was running, after only a couple of months—or was it less?—living in the state. The inevitable howls of carpetbagging at first meant nothing because Ortagus had the support of none other than Donald J. Trump. Not long thereafter, Grenell quietly (almost silently) withdrew his support from Starbuck and announced for the onetime spokeswoman to former secretary of state Mike Pompeo.

How did this all happen? Rumors flew about a visit to Mar-a-Lago by Ortagus and her powerful political adviser/manager Ward Baker, a man known as the local Karl Rove but whose influence extended well beyond the state and threatened to supersede Rove's. I wasn't supposed to like Ward because of his backroom reputation, but I did. I always found him to be an engaging fellow when I met with him. He was the key adviser to Marsha Blackburn but also to National Republican Senatorial Committee chair Roger Wicker, who said that "Hiring Ward was one of the best political decisions I've ever made."

No doubt it was, but on this particular Palm Beach excursion Baker appears to have had a great deal of even more powerful help. Ortagus, an attractive woman, was buddies with the fashionable Ivanka Trump and, again according to rumor, was introduced and recommended to the former president by his favored daughter.

Almost immediately the former Pompeo spox was anointed as Trump's candidate in the Fifth. Don Jr., who is said to have preferred Robby Starbuck, objected but to no apparent avail, as his father publicly proclaimed Ortagus a distinguished foreign policy expert who would make a great contribution to the Congress and would, of course, be MAGA or even ultra-MAGA (whatever that was), although she had not so long ago been an adamant Never Trumper and had blasted Trump as "disgusting" as recently as 2016 on CNN.

That was only the first of the many twists and turns to come. Trump—either beguiled by a pretty face, anxious to please his daughter, or, if you prefer a more Machiavellian interpretation, taking the opportunity to outflank his possible competitor Pompeo by co-opting his spokeswoman—had not gambled on local pushback (or if he did, he didn't care). But that pushback was strong. A bill was enacted in the Tennessee Assembly and eventually signed by Governor Bill Lee that would preclude anyone from running in a primary who hadn't lived in the state for at least three years. It was aimed straight at Ortagus, and to some extent at Starbuck.

The man who initiated this legislation was State Senator Frank Niceley. Niceley told Nashville News Channel 5, "We don't want carpetbaggers coming in here with lots of money. I mean if you've got star quality and money, you can win. Money usually turns into votes, and we don't want people coming in here and buying these seats. We want representation in Congress that understands, not only which interstates come into Nashville, but understands our culture—our Southern culture."

Niceley's reference to interstates was a not-so-subtle knock on Ortagus, who, during a recent appearance on Leahy's radio show, was asked by the host if she could name any of the several interstate highways that encircle and cut through Nashville and were used by most of the city's commuters on a daily basis. She couldn't think of one. It was as if a Los Angeleno drew a blank on the Hollywood and Ventura Freeways—not a great look if you were running for office in the area. Things were not going well for Ortagus. But then, Senator Niceley left himself open to a pack of embarrassment. Niceley is the representative of Strawberry Plains, a whistlestop three hours and ten minutes east of Nashville on the I-40, the major US highway that runs 2,556 miles from Barstow, California, to Wilmington, North Carolina, and connects three of Tennessee's major cities: Memphis, Nashville, and Knoxville. In the flush of the victory of his bill's passage, he clumsily sought to make amends with Trump and his followers during an interview: "I think Jared Kushner—he's Jewish, she's Jewish—I think Jared will be upset. Ivanka will be upset. I don't think Trump cares."

Oops. Had Niceley gone racist redneck, invalidating his cause of "Tennessee First" by attacking Ortagus (whom some had been calling a "Gucci-bagger" rather than a "carpetbagger") with one of the world's oldest calumnies? Ortagus converted to her husband's Judaism while in Saudi Arabia, of all places, working for Pompeo. No synagogues existed in that country, of course, so she studied with a rabbi online. Perhaps she was a harbinger of the Israeli–Saudi rapprochement working its way through reluctant old-school holdovers in the Saudi hierarchy and now seeming to have run afoul under the Biden administration. Or perhaps she was imitating friend Ivanka, who had similarly converted to her husband Jared's Judaism. Or maybe, just maybe, there was authentic conviction in her religious conversion. (Although rare, such things happen in politics.) In any case, Ortagus took the opportunity to respond to Niceley with outrage that may or may not have been more than political: "Anti-Semitism is the oldest and one of the most vile forms of hatred on this earth, and Sen. Niceley should be ashamed of his repeated anti-Semitic rhetoric," she said in a statement. "I am incredibly proud to call myself a part of the Jewish people, and I have always called out anti-Semitism when I see it in all of its forms. I will condemn anyone who traffics in this hate-mongering. Sen. Niceley's repulsive words could not be more clear in disparaging the Jewish people. This racism cannot stand."

Niceley responded: "In an extended interview with NBC News, a reporter decided to take a small portion of my comments out of context in order to manufacture a controversy to distract people from the fact that Morgan Ortagus was declared ineligible for the ballot by both the Tennessee Republican Party and the General Assembly. Let me be clear: I have nothing but respect for the Jewish people and the State of Israel. Attempting to construe my off-hand comments about the Trump family as antisemitism is unfair and inaccurate."

His comment was dumb, undoubtedly, but antisemitic? Not so clear.

And so it went, Ortagus appearing on *The View* (always sympathetic to any possible Republican-bashing) to redouble her accusations. Some speculated she would be on a plane back to DC in a matter of days, her Tennessee sojourn an unfortunate few months' interlude on a shining résumé. But she hung on, finding another candidate to back in the Fifth: a retired National Guard brigadier general named Kurt Winstead. It was an odd choice, since Winstead's wife was a Democrat lobbyist and Winstead himself would prove to be, to put it kindly, intellectually challenged as well as purposefully deceptive as the campaign wore on. Those revelations only gave credence to the State Executive Committee of the Republican Party's decision (13–3, exactly the same as the vote against Starbuck) to deny Ortagus's own candidacy.

The deliberations of the unpaid committee are conducted in private. Some complained about the lack of transparency, but, as with almost everything in politics, word leaks out. In the case of Starbuck, the committee was reportedly disturbed by a multiplicity of matters, including his lying and the rap videos he produced and directed only months before moving from California to Tennessee. The videos were borderline pornographic—an odd set of projects for someone who, when he arrived in Tennessee, immediately promoted himself as the defender of children in the schools. This would be the man to purify the educational system and return it to its constitutional roots, away from the wokeness invading so many red states despite a citizenry that almost uniformly rejected it? He would save these citizens?

Starbuck was, unfortunately, the wrong messenger, but a charismatic one—more charismatic than most of his adversaries in the Tennessee Fifth. He decided to continue on as a write-in candidate and retained a surprising number of followers via his favored method of communication, Instagram. In a sense, he had no choice. Starbuck had gone "all-in," jetting around the country to collect campaign support from all manner of celebrities, political and otherwise. What could he tell them now? What could he tell himself?

All this had turned a relatively minor Tennessee congressional election into something of a national cause. I had little idea, at that point, the degree to which my wife and I would be plunged into the middle of the debate to come. I was also unaware of how much I had to learn about the nature of Southern politics—everyone's politics, really. Given the amount of ineptitude, self-interest, and dishonesty, it's a miracle we have survived as a country. ∎

17

YARD SIGN POLITICS

Election season in America basically revolves around yard signs, dumb as that sounds on the slightest reflection. You know it's election time when the signs begin to sprout on every lawn as if they were a new, deer-resistant variant of hydrangea. Count them up and you'll know who's the winner. Of course, that's a ridiculous way to see elections, but that's the way many candidates and their supporters did, particularly in the smaller elections and even in many larger ones. The bigger the signs, the bigger the candidate—or something. Trump signs were naturally one of the great targets of our time, either to swipe or deface. Get your spray cans ready and try to remember in which direction swastikas were drawn.

This is not unique to the South, of course, but one especially farcical episode not far from my Nashville neighborhood began when a man either quit or was fired as campaign manager for a woman running for the state assembly. For some unknown reason, this woman had convinced two different friends of hers to compete for the same position on the aforementioned GOP State Executive Committee. She therefore ended up having yard signs for both on her property, separated, not surprisingly, by a larger one for herself. She was also involved with some kind of hushed-up lawsuit over illegal political robocalls concerning a property tax increase, and she was mired in mind-boggling political squabbles between people who had not an inch of actual ideological difference.

Confused yet? Me too. Anyway, this woman won the primary surprisingly easily and probably deserved it for running a more energetic campaign. It was also rumored, however, that she had a dark side, via another lawsuit regarding a possible scandal years ago that she had to settle. Whether her Democrat opponent was aware of this is unknown, but it was moot. She lost the general election in a district that had been carved out for the Republicans to win.

But back to the man who either was fired or quit. He decided to run for the SEC himself and got into a mess that wasn't only about yard signs, but was what you might call yard-sign-related—or yard-sign-adjacent, as the realtors might say. The incident went public and was the cause of some consternation, as well as some laughter, among the refugees and the rank-and-file. The *Tennessee Star*'s Aaron Guldbrandsen described the humiliating situation succinctly: "He was caught by a Ring doorbell camera stealing his opponent's campaign literature and replacing it with his own."

The man in question, John Richardson, issued an apology on Facebook that reads in part,

> While knocking on doors and meeting voters I came across my opponent's campaign literature and another candidate's literature at a door. Based on the way the literature was stuffed into the door handle I assumed that my opponent was working with another candidate. I was told by the other candidate that they were not going to play favorites in my race, and in a moment of deep heartbreak I made an emotional decision that I regret. I removed the campaign literature from someone's door, so that I could bring it home to show my wife. I have apologized to both my opponent and the other candidate and I am now asking for the forgiveness from my supporters. My opponent is a good man, and if you choose to vote for him because of this event,

I completely understand. I am also requesting your grace be extended to me. My momentary, uncharacteristic lapse in judgment requires that I re-establish your trust. I will be grateful for your understanding and forgiveness.

Whatever one might think of the "deep heartbreak" involved in the competition for this (I remind you) unpaid office, Richardson was still elected and has been, I am told, a more than decent member of the SEC.

But the local skullduggery afoot—candidates lying, cheating, and stealing for such minor positions—has been replicated on the far larger scale of our national politics. The current president of the United States himself was caught plagiarizing in law school, of all places, and then, after promising never to do it again, continued to do it several times thereafter, stealing the words of other major politicians. Is it any wonder that such a person would leave top-secret documents strewn willy-nilly around his garage? And then there are the little matters of the Durham Report and the revelation of millions of dollars for his family from China and Romania by a House committee. But those are the subjects of what will undoubtedly be many other books.

Richardson, to be fair, was a self-starter, and he did run hard for this voluntary service. He made an effort to improve things in his way, even if that meant stealing his opponent's campaign literature. That was more than you could say for the virtually useless Davidson County Republican Party, whose then-chairman—an irascible fellow more than a little past his prime, who in that sense (distantly) resembled Biden and who has also been accused of skulking about in the middle of the night cutting up yard signs—made little or no attempt to find Republican candidates except for a couple of friends to run against Democrats in that blue city. Few did run.

Inexplicably, for instance, Republicans didn't even put up a candidate for Nashville's new district attorney, a job that is arguably more important than mayor in our crime-ridden times. This was a baffling concession to the Democrats, especially because Nashville, for reasons that seem to point back to the old days of Southern corruption, has a unique (as far as I know) eight-year term for DA. Many kings didn't last that long. The chairman of the county Republicans apparently didn't care. He spent his time writing late-night emails playing favorites in party elections, when such behavior was forbidden for a party official, and smearing anyone who threatened his position or even wanted mildly to reform the inept group. No wonder Tennessee Republicans have made few inroads in their state capital in years. I wondered to what degree this defeatist and narcissistic behavior was duplicated by local Republican leadership elsewhere. I suspected it was significant. (Thankfully, a new, more competent DCRP chair has recently been elected.)

Such is the nature of what I call "political lust," because it implies a less controlled and much wilder impulse than the traditional term "power hungry."

The woman running for state assembly suffered from a clear case of political lust, daffily urging two of her friends to run for the same office she once held herself, as if everyone should want their turn at the poker table. It's what one did. It came as no surprise that she ultimately lost the election for state assembly.

I saw this same unruly impulse in some of the cross-country migrants too, even though it was often channeled to a better cause, as the groups split because of ideological differences so minute it would have taken a Talmudic scholar even to begin to parse them. Collaboration might have been a better way, but political lust is a communicable disease, and if you are from California, or New York or Chicago for that matter, you spent a good portion of your life surrounded by people with considerable, often overwhelming, lust. Sometimes this was political lust, sometimes artistic lust, sometimes financial lust, sometimes regular-old sexual lust, and sometimes it was all of the above mashed together at once. All of these cities are capitals of unremitting competition. So, no matter who you were, you carried at least some of these impulses with you to your new home. I know I did. Sometimes it helped me and sometimes it didn't. Sometimes I tried to shake off this constant drumbeat of desire, this need to stand out in some way, but it was in my DNA. You have to eat a lot of shrimp and grits to become a genuine Southerner. And then you find out that some of the DNA stored in that very soul food has only a slightly different configuration. A Tennessean, if he or she wanted to, could be as mean-spirited as any Yankee. It came down to a difference of accent. ■

18

THE TEACHINGS OF ROCKY TOP: PART ONE

Roger Simon: "Which is worse? State politics or national politics?"

Rocky Top: "National. At least locally we know our limitations and adjust expectations accordingly."

At first, I wondered if that was correct. We were in the midst of the 2022 primary season in Tennessee, and I was witnessing—largely through my wife Sheryl Longin, who had become first vice president of the Nashville Republican Women—more backbiting and skullduggery among people who were supposed to be on the same side than you might have found in Renaissance Florence. The situation could be described as low-rent Medici, or even opéra bouffe. I know that to say this is about as far from politically correct as you can get, but this behavior seemed to be especially predominant in women. Men would compete for all they were worth in a game of basketball or tennis, but when it was over, it was over. Off for a beer. Women never took the shiv out of their sister's back, twisting and turning it, it seemed, as long as humanly possible. These days, however, they did so via an unending series of texts and emails that could be just as nasty, in their way, as a knife—and more long-lasting. Digital was forever.

But my above analysis, that local politics were as dastardly and vicious as national—was written only days before the FBI staged their early-morning raid on Donald Trump's Mar-a-Lago compound, rummaging among his effects (and those of Melania Trump's and sixteen-year-old Baron) in a fishing expedition that went on for hours, his lawyers forbidden from observing. This intrusion, which called to mind Stalin's security chief Lavrentiy Beria's "Show me the man and I will show you the crime," crossed an American Rubicon. Many were saying that our democratic republic had developed into a banana republic.

When I asked Rocky Top, via text, whether he thought this event marked the end of the USA as we knew it, he answered in typical gnomic fashion: "TBD—could go either way."

Indeed, it could.

His earlier point about national politics was well taken. It had a brutal impersonality. And it seemed to be getting worse.

Getting to Rocky Top meant a complicated trip through parts of the state I had never seen. As I drove past gorgeous rolling hills with cattle lingering under the shade of giant oaks, the humid weather neared a hundred degrees. After turning down what I thought more than once was the end of the road, I finally found his property, which encompassed several acres. This included a handful of buildings—windswept, sun-bleached, and lived-in. These buildings had age, but they looked comfortable in the way people used to call "old shoe." I wouldn't have minded spending time there myself. There were houses I had lived in that were similar, but on considerably less acreage. The land itself was magnificent, but all land was beautiful in that part of Middle Tennessee. Even abandoned gas stations had their appeal.

I later learned Rocky had bought the place online after only two hours, without ever seeing it, when, fed up with the Beltway world after decades (being an adviser to presidents and presidential candidates was evidently not all it was cracked up to be), he finally decided to decamp from DC and return to his native Tennessee.

I also learned that the small wooden building next to which I had parked—nearly a decrepit shack, really—was a former slave quarters. I can't say I took that news with equanimity. How could you live with the presence of such a thing on your property? It was perhaps only a hundred feet from what I discovered was the main house. Why wasn't it bulldozed ages ago?

I was similarly perplexed that the suburban Nashville street I drove down several times a week to play tennis was still named Robert E. Lee Drive (or "Robert East Lee Drive," according to the voice of my GPS). Although the street's identification signs were sometimes bent back or defaced, the drive itself remained named after the commander of the Army of Northern Virginia, the most successful of all Southern armies during the Civil War. Another street nearby was still named for Jefferson Davis, the first and only president of the Confederate States of America. Another in that neighborhood was called Confederate Drive. I considered whether these things should be removed, but in the end I opposed such actions, remembering of the opening lines of L. P. Hartley's *The Go-Between*: "The past is a foreign country: they do things differently there."

I don't know if Rocky Top is as much a fan of the British novelist as I am—I wouldn't be surprised—but he told me a story that explained the value he saw in keeping that slave house up.

He had once been visited by a lawyer friend from Chattanooga, a black man who came with his ten-year-old son. While he and the lawyer talked, the boy wandered over to the shack and peered inside.

"What's this?" he called out.

"The old slave quarters," Rocky told me he replied. I wondered how he felt at that moment.

The young boy instantly sprung backward as if he had seen a ghost.

"No, no. Go in," said the boy's father. "It won't bite you. You should see it...I'll join you."

And he did. Father and son, both black, entered the old slave quarters that Rocky Top said was now being used as a tool shed. He also said that at this point he retreated a distance, allowing the pair inside the shack to have their space to deal with whatever thoughts came up. After a while they came out again and resumed conversation on other matters, as if nothing had happened. But something obviously changed. Rocky suspected that it had helped them, and particularly the boy, make some peace, to the extent they could, at least for now, with the horrific treatment of their people.

To deny that enduring history, to pretend it had not happened or to believe that it will ever be fully resolved, is to be living in some kind of dream. Everywhere you go in Middle Tennessee you are met with reminders of slavery and the Civil War in the form of bronze sign markers that explain what happened at that location. (A smarter way to deal with all the statues would have been: leave them in place, accompanied by full explanations who these people were and what they did.) The same club where I play tennis has an adjoining luxe and elaborate new golf course that was the site of the Battle of Nashville, in which an estimated six thousand died. A sign by the gate to the club makes this clear. By comparison, they say 2,400 American servicemen died in the whole Afghanistan war. The Civil War was America's bloodiest.

Rocky Top was no racist. He was from an abolitionist family from way back, always Republican, a proud member of the party of Lincoln. He grew up in a sparsely populated valley close to what is now called Oak Ridge, the nuclear weapons research redoubt that, as I mentioned, was my first connection to Tennessee through my father. Oak Ridge was chosen for its proximity to the newly built Tennessee Valley Authority and thus readily available power, and also because the area was inland, away from the coasts and the attendant risks of foreign espionage.

Rocky Top's father was involved in all this, as was mine—a bit of kismet that emerged as we swapped stories. His father was a blue-collar worker, a machinist working unhappily in "Yankee"

Baltimore ("Yankee" to them anyway) when a government man approached him to see if he would be interested in a job in Tennessee. He jumped at the chance to return home without even asking what the job was, although the government man, evidently FBI, knew no more himself than that the job was for a machinist. When Rocky Top *père* arrived back in Tennessee, he was astonished to find his destination was his own tiny home region, which had been renamed and grown into a burgeoning town of seventy thousand. He was given instructions to machine a pipe about a yard long but was not told to what end. He apparently did not learn the full scope of the project—that he had been building part of the firing mechanism for the first atomic bomb to be used in war, "Little Boy"—until a few days after it fell on Hiroshima. He must have done a good job, because he worked for many years thereafter as a machinist on top-secret nuclear weapons projects in Oak Ridge.

It's impossible to say if he ever knew my father (both men are dead), but he could have. Norman Simon, a radiologist who treated the "Hiroshima maidens" after the bomb, traveled every month from New York City to Oak Ridge to give his medical opinion on the effects of human exposure to the latest nuclear weaponry. He would return to our Manhattan apartment after a few days, ashen-faced from the horrific capabilities of what he had seen. It was the 1950s, and thoughts of Herman Kahn's thermonuclear war were topping the unthinkable agenda.

Oak Ridge, a mysterious, faraway place where scientists congregated to devise frightening inventions, was my childhood introduction to Tennessee. For Rocky Top, it was more or less home.

I got to know him first as a blogger at his website sonsofrockytop.com, which had the words "WE. ARE. BACK." at the very top, written in precisely that manner. He apparently had another blog some years ago called rockytoppolitics.com, but had taken a hiatus.

The intention of both blogs was not to go viral and become a public sensation, but to be something of a private nuisance, to speak the unpopular truth to an audience of roughly five hundred Tennesseans, largely politicians, the ones who determine the future of the state. Rocky Top's writerly voice was snarky, a bit vicious, and honest. It was also funny, as the take-no-prisoners approach often is. He did this all, as noted, anonymously, in an effort to generate interest from his target audience. His goal was to break the omertà, the code of supposedly polite but actually self-serving silence that engulfs the upper reaches of American politics, not just in Tennessee but in virtually all fifty states and, above all, in Washington, DC.

Apparently, it worked. There was buzz around the site. Rocky Top gored all oxen—not just those in power but also the incoming political wannabes among the arriving migrants. I had been introduced to the blog via the ongoing debate over two of those wannabes, the charismatic Robby Starbuck and the well-connected Morgan Ortagus. Rocky made short work of them under such headlines as: "Starbuck: 'Stop Telling the Truth About Me or I Will Sue!'" and "We Have Met the Swamp and the Swamp Is Morgan Ortagus." Nastier was "Is Morgan Ortagus Smarter than a Williamson County 6th Grader?" after the branded "Gucci-bagger" couldn't answer the most elementary questions about her new home state. When both candidates were deemed unqualified for the ballot by the party committee, Rocky unleashed the succinct "Man Bun Down!" for the bun-clad Robby and a copy of Southwest Airlines flight times from Nashville back to Washington for Morgan, anticipating her imminent return to DC (though, as mentioned, she ended up staying, for the nonce anyway).

Rocky was not, however, biased against newcomers in general—only these particular newcomers. He was an equal-opportunity destroyer with unkind—others might say accurate but impolite—things to say about many important Tennessee public figures, from Governor Bill Lee down. Rocky Top, although having been deep in the swamps of both DC and Tennessee, was on the side of the outsiders, a.k.a. the People. By sticking it to the insiders, he had the outsiders' welfare at heart, even if few outsiders ever read a word he said.

Anyway, the day I had lunch with him for our second meeting, we both agreed that the world had changed so radically in the last twenty-four hours that our minor differences—and they were minor—had become irrelevant, almost trivial, and barely worth commenting on. Tip O'Neill's "all politics is local" was no more. All politics was local, national, and international all at once and mixed together as never before—and not just because the internet now told you within seconds what was going on in Kuala Lumpur. That was information, however dreadful, you could ignore. Not this.

The FBI, acting for all intents and purposes like the Soviet NKVD, had broken into Donald Trump's estate in Palm Beach, Mar-a-Lago. ∎

19

A COLD CIVIL WAR

Everything was in the air now, from secession to civil war. I realized that those questions would hang over this book. The migrants, the American refugees—whatever you wanted to call them—were now at the very center of history, testing whether our nation could "long endure."

I texted Olivia Shupe, whom I had come to regard as my window into the best of the refugee world. "Do you and your husband think we are headed for secession or civil war?"

I almost immediately got back this response: "Yes probably. We were just listening to a podcast on this. The whistleblower was talking about how 6.2 million encrypted emails [were] being sent back and forth about civil war in the last few weeks."

In the midst of the Mar-a-Lago break-in and even before, Victor Davis Hanson, generally acknowledged to be the dean of contemporary conservative pundits, was saying we were in a "revolutionary cycle." This comported with the response I got from Rocky Top, whom I also asked if we were headed for secession and/or civil war. I had requested that he respond pithily, but I got back a prediction that was far more developed and serious:

Not a formal secession/civil war, but a slow, smoldering revolt between the states. Increase in rates of out-migration, individual acts of protest like bussing migrants to DC, removing law enforcement cooperation with the Feds, more 10th Amendment battles, etc. Great example just this week: Arizona using shipping containers to plug holes in the Wall. All of this could move along slowly but have potential of exploding into something larger. The Left hasn't learned a damn thing. They will continue to intensify their push to punish the normally passive Right—looking to create incidents they can use as an excuse to ramp up their authoritarian push. Sorry, I am feeling decidedly un-pithy these days.

So was I. And pithy or not, this seemed a good summation of where we were, with the Department of Justice doing everything it could to hide the affidavit that was supposed to justify the Mar-a-Lago break-in, which Trump insisted was a witch hunt to obtain the Russiagate documents.

And yet I was nervous. I would be satisfied with a slow-motion secession. It was better than millions of corpses. But somehow, I wondered if that could finally happen. We were evidently in some kind of cold civil war. The Left was ruthless in its attempt to take over the country by any means necessary, while the Right did little more than complain about it on social media, which was itself largely the province of the Left until Elon Musk purchased Twitter.

The angry Left needn't have worried about Musk. They continue to have an ironclad grip on the flow of information, for their own believing audience and for too much of our own, from Facebook to the *New York Times* to the Associated Press to government-licensed television networks ABC, NBC, and CBS. We—even those of us who escaped blue states to red states like Tennessee, where the local news is a pathetic parody of the national—are living in an amped-up version of that famous quote attributed to everyone from Mark

Twain to Winston Churchill: "A lie can travel halfway around the globe before the truth can get its boots on." In our high-tech world, with that lie going around at the speed of light, the only way to contradict it would be to sleep with your boots on.

Despite his pessimistic outlook, Rocky Top in his way was showing more ultimate belief in the survival of a constitutional republic than I had. But these things change by the minute, like the capricious, fast-moving Tennessee weather. ∎

20

QU'EST-CE QUE C'EST
UNE FEMME?

The same night I received Rocky's text message, I attended the debut of *What Is a Woman?*, a new, exceptionally well-constructed documentary made by the Daily Wire's Matt Walsh. The real subject beneath the question posed by the title was the plague of sexual reassignment surgery and puberty blockers sweeping through our country and the West in general. This epidemic was spreading like a wildfire, largely among the young. These youths were encouraged by experts—psychiatrists, pediatricians, teachers, and so forth—but decidedly not by their parents. It was arguably the most extreme form of child abuse yet devised, but it was widely welcomed by the self-described woke and the many who follow or fear them. It had hit Tennessee, specifically its vaunted Vanderbilt University Medical Center, with a vengeance.

Attending the premiere of the film at the historic Franklin Theatre were what might be described as *le tout Tennessee conservateur*, including both natives and refugees. The natives were mostly politicians from the state assembly and business stalwarts—at least those not already infected by that other epidemic, "Environmental, Social, and Governance" (ESG). The refugees, a smaller but still significant group, were activists or involved in the Daily Wire, which had only recently moved from Los Angeles to Nashville. Also in attendance was Senator Marsha Blackburn, who had been approached by the filmmakers after asking that same simple question—"What is a woman?"—of Supreme Court nominee Ketanji Brown Jackson, receiving as an answer the kind of non-sensical pseudo-intellectual blather only a graduate of Harvard could come up with.

Before the documentary, Walsh, Blackburn, and producer/director Justin Folk came up to introduce the film. Walsh told the audience that his documentary did not aspire to solve the problem, only to expose it, which it did very well. He said there would be time to discuss possible solutions during the scheduled Q&A after the screening, and he implored attendees to do so.

It didn't happen. Not a single question—almost all of which were asked by the politicians or businesspeople—remotely addressed solutions. Though effusively complimentary of the film, the questions themselves were inane and pointless, as if those asking had not heard what Walsh requested in his introduction.

This underscored my view that had grown consistently over my time in Tennessee, that most of the politicians and the business community on the right were immune to solutions, as if they had an allergy to actually doing anything that might disturb the status quo and effectuate positive change.

Instead, it was if by attending the film they had done enough. You see, we care. But don't ask us to do something about it. That would offend Big Pharma, which was making a stupendous fortune from these gender treatments, just as it did from the pandemic. Besides, Big Pharma, in tandem with Big Tech, are our biggest financial backers.

This all, of course, went unspoken. Yet it was the nub of the problem in many, if not most, red states. In blue states, where Big

Pharma runs amuck with hardly any resistance, they barely even reach the "we care" level. Let the children have fun changing sexes a half dozen times; let them even commit suicide after taking puberty blockers whose results and impact on the brain no one remotely understands. It's an important social experiment. And don't bother telling us that the distributor of Lupron, among the most common of those blockers, lost a lawsuit of over $800 million when it was found to be giving kickbacks to doctors to prescribe it. That was back in 2002; the drug has a new distributor now.

The exploitation, actually the encouragement, of the transgender epidemic under the guise of helping adolescents find their true selves is an atrocity that could be prevented by political leaders on the state and national levels. But these politicians never do, for fear of alienating the very font of their campaign contributions. Instead they suffer from another sort of epidemic, one equally if not more debilitating: cowardice.

Only the people themselves, in this case a very wealthy portion thereof, seem able to do something about this. The same month Walsh's film premiered, the parents of the Nashville private girls' school Harpeth Hall rose up almost as one against the school's faculty and administration, which had gone so woke that they had banned George Washington Day, were teaching American history as a series of evil atrocities, and began encouraging boys who were transitioning to girls to attend the school and use the girls' bathrooms. The appalled parents, some of whom were on the board of directors, were able to engineer a complete reversal and have faculty and administrators fired. This was a good first step, obviously, but one that did nothing for the much greater number of kids attending public schools throughout the state, whose families' values were similarly being trampled underfoot.

Where were the state politicians in all this? Nowhere to be seen, except perhaps to tut-tut for the record. Of course, in the blue states they would be cheering it on. With a little luck, the cumbersome past—the legacy of Western Civilization, the Judeo-Christian tradition, etc.—would be gone and a new (or is it old?) form of government would be born (or reborn).

Or is it already here? ■

21

GEORGIA, THE WRONG WAY SOUTH

One of the intentions of this book is to provide potential refugees with a kind of *Fodor's* guide to red states to help them make their choice. It will be perforce incomplete. I live in Tennessee, and you only really know what a place is like—and then "through a glass darkly"—if you've lived in or otherwise spent a sufficient amount of time in that place. Therefore, too, since I know more of Tennessee, I know more of its negative side, but that doesn't mean it's the worst place to go. It's probably, in all, one of the better ones, and not just because of those bucolic vistas.

However, if there were one red state I would tell you not to move to, one that I have visited a number of times, it would be Georgia. It's not really a red state anymore. It is said to be purple. But is it really even that? It is sui generis, something of its own sort. But it's not good, and augurs poorly for the future.

Yes, I am aware that there are many wonderful people in Georgia— I've met a number of them—and interesting and beautiful places to visit. But something happened to the state, or rather didn't happen, because if there is any place that embodies the Old South politically, the world of the reviled Southern Democrats with Jim Crow unresolved on all sides, it is Georgia—only those Democrats, the ones in power anyway, now appear on the ballot as Republicans. And those appearing on the ballot as Democrats are exactly the same thing, the creepiest of hypocrites exploiting the public at any turn for personal financial benefit.

Worst of all is the city of Atlanta—a giant urban sprawl similar to Los Angeles but without the glamour, Hollywood history, or even the great museums most international cities have. On the plus side, they don't seem to have LA's homelessness problem yet, but violence is everywhere. You don't want to walk the sidewalks at night between the glittering high-rises of the upscale Buckhead neighborhood. With a few exceptions, people aren't even safe at the fanciest malls.

I don't know how all this evolved, although I can make some guesses. I experienced it personally on trips down to Atlanta covering the 2020 presidential campaign and later senatorial campaigns. As in so many states, there appeared to be two Republican parties: the first a party of so-called elites (officials and business leaders); the other a party of the people (the middle class, the working class, and small business owners). The latter party, however, seemed able to make even fewer inroads here than elsewhere. This was true despite the dramatic (and sometimes melodramatic) rallying cries of attorneys Sidney Powell and Lin Wood.

I attended one of their rallies in a suburb of Atlanta that promised considerably more than it delivered. It was the first time since the arrival of Covid-19 that I was in a large crowd; there were around two or three thousand people, with barely a mask to be seen. As far as I could tell, almost no one in attendance had moved to Georgia during the migrant wave. There were a number of disaffected Georgians present, plus people who had driven from nearby states like Florida and Tennessee, and even farther afield. I talked to one person who came from Arizona but was happy to remain there, battling, as she said, for election reform with the powers that be in her volatile home. Still, the mood that day was optimistic, hoping for something Sidney Powell called "The Kraken," definitive proof of voter fraud in the 2020 presidential election. It never materialized—at least from Powell.

Around the same time I attended a Senate runoff election night party of the establishment Republican Party at one of the luxe hotels in Buckhead. It was a very different crowd, well dressed, gossiping while indulging in cocktails and hors d'oeuvres. Not much attention was paid to the returns being projected on a large screen, because things were not looking good for their candidate, Kelly Loeffler, in her race against Raphael Warnock, despite the accusations of spousal abuse against Warnock. That Loeffler's husband was the CEO of Intercontinental Exchange—a company that owns and operates a dozen financial exchanges and marketplaces across the globe—probably had not helped the hoary negative reputation of Republicans as the party of big business. Nor did the appearances of Governor Brian Kemp and Georgia Secretary of State Brad Raffensperger when I was introduced to them that night. At first glance they seemed like the manager and salesman of the local Mercedes dealership. As they gripped my hand, pretending to be pleased to meet me while they looked around the room, H. L. Mencken's apothegm "When somebody says it's not about the money, it's about the money" rattled through my brain. (Not coincidently, Kemp was one of the few Republicans to join the billionaire globalists at that conspiracy against the common man, the World Economic Forum in Davos, Switzerland, January 2023.) I wondered too if they knew that I had just attended a meeting run by activists who swore that they, Kemp and Raffensperger, had thrown the presidential election in Georgia to Biden.

I couldn't get solid evidence from this activist group—not solid enough, anyway. Yet there also wasn't the slightest evidence that it *hadn't* been stolen. American elections had long been constructed so no one could really be sure of their true outcomes. This applied to all fifty states.

Elections in the USA are an unholy mess, and the refugees knew it. It was one of their greatest concerns and ultimately the most frustrating, because they were up against a status quo that was unimaginably powerful. Every time they raised an issue about the election, they were brushed back by the powers that be.

Blame corruption, blame bureaucracy; even the US Census has its problems. If we don't know how many we are, then how can we possibly have free and fair elections? As Hans von Spakovsky of the Heritage Foundation writes,

> In a shocking report, the U.S. Census Bureau recently admitted that it overcounted the populations of eight states and under-counted the populations of six states in the 2020 census...Those costly errors will distort congressional representation and the Electoral College. It means that when the Census Bureau reapportioned the House of Representatives, Florida was cheated out of two additional seats it should have gotten; Texas missed out on another seat; Minnesota and Rhode Island each kept a representative they shouldn't have; and Colorado was awarded a new member of the House it didn't deserve.

According to this post-census survey, Texas was undercounted by a staggering 560,319 residents. Was this a product of their open border? How many more have slipped in since? Double that? Quadruple that? No one knows. No one knows who's voting either. Based on a percentage of population, red Arkansas was the most undercounted state at 5.04 percent. Tennessee and Mississippi were also undercounted. Sense a pattern?

None of this matters to the establishment as long as the right people, what the French call bon chic, bon genre (BCBG), get into office. On the surface, BCBG seems to have changed in this era of the woke, but has it really? Stacey Abrams, repeatedly the

Democratic contender for the same Georgia governorship, claimed to be a victim time and time again. Really, she was just another privileged Yalie hoping to convince others of her victimhood for personal gain.

In Georgia, recently, we have seen the exceptionally lavish remarriage of liberal Hollywood celebrities Ben Affleck and Jennifer Lopez at Affleck's eighty-seven-acre mock-antebellum compound outside Savannah. It wasn't that long ago (2015) that writer/director/actor Affleck was doing his best to obscure his family's own slaveholding antebellum past on Harvard's Henry Louis Gates's *Finding Your Roots* show on PBS. This was 2022, and by now the actor had paid sufficient penance, mouthing the requisite left-wing pieties that enabled him to live in the grand manner of his ancestors and then some, except that he would have to pay his copious staff for their work.

To be fair, I can understand Affleck's romance with the South, if not the excessive manner in which he lived it out. Despite its old reputation, Los Angeles was the least laid back—therefore the least relaxing or comforting—place in America, the constant drumbeat of competitiveness never stopping as cars whiz by on the Hollywood Freeway. It even beats New York in that regard. Who wouldn't want to flee Los Angeles as often as possible, even before its recent epidemic of homelessness and crime?

It should also go without saying that there are great people in Georgia, such as the aforementioned Garland Favorito of VoterGA, with whom I sat at the State Farm Arena when votes were counted and then counted again but which somehow never added up. People like Favorito and Kathleen Harms in Tennessee are the heroes of our times. But they were the exceptions, similar in some ways to the lamed Vav in the Jewish tradition—the thirty-six righteous people who save the world for the next generation. The number thirty-six comes from Hebrew mystic numerology and seems insufficient for today's global population of seven billion, but people like this deserve to be praised and nurtured wherever they are. They are surpassingly rare.

Why, I wondered, could the people of Georgia, and those of practically every other state in our country, not shake free of their execrable leadership on both sides of the aisle? How could the people actually stand for such pervasive mediocrity? The answer may simply be that no decent person would dare run for office in the climate of today's America, only to have every mistake they may or may not have made in their lives dredged up and replayed endlessly to the world.

But that doesn't explain the docility, the mass sheepishness, of the public, which in many parts of America had come to resemble Germany's Weimar Republic. It wasn't just Georgia. Across the country, in almost every state, the majority, or nearly, were complying with the status quo. Why?

Some time ago, a quote from the eighteenth-century Scottish essayist Alexander Tytler appeared in the comments section of an article I had written on Joe Biden's student loan tax forgiveness plan.

> A democracy cannot exist as a permanent form of government. It can only exist until the voters discover that they can vote themselves largesse from the public treasury. From that moment on, the majority always votes for the candidates promising the most benefits from the public treasury with the result that a democracy always collapses over loose fiscal policy, always followed by a dictatorship.

If that was where we were headed, was there a point in being a refugee, American or otherwise? Did it even matter where we were? Since change was so seemingly impossible, should we just relax and try as best we could to enjoy what little freedom we still had? Or did it mean the time had come to fight harder? An unknown author put the conundrum this way, with frightening eloquence:

> The most terrifying force of death, comes from the hands of Men who wanted to be left Alone. They try, so very hard, to mind their own business and provide for themselves and those they love.
>
> They resist every impulse to fight back, knowing the forced and permanent change of life that will come from it. They know, that the moment they fight back, their lives as they have lived them, are over.
>
> The moment the Men who wanted to be left alone are forced to fight back, it is a form of suicide. They are literally killing off who they used to be. Which is why, when forced to take up violence, these Men who wanted to be left alone, fight with unholy vengeance against those who murdered their former lives. They fight with raw hate, and a drive that cannot be fathomed by those who are merely play-acting at politics and terror. True terror will arrive at these people's door, and they will cry, scream, and beg for mercy...but it will fall upon the deaf ears of the Men who just wanted to be left alone.

Did we refugees want to be left alone, or did we migrate across the country with a not-so-hidden intention to fight? It depended on the day.

It might be worth interjecting at this point something that I learned for the first time at Passover 2023 (5783 on the Jewish calendar), which I celebrated with my wife and daughter at Chabad of Nashville. I have not been able to get it out of my mind since. Rashi, the medieval French rabbi and among the most renowned of all Talmudic scholars, wrote that only twenty percent of the Jews agreed to take the risk of following Moses out of Egypt during the Exodus. The rest—the vast majority—preferred to remain as slaves to Pharoah.

If true, and I suspect it largely is, this tells us a lot about human behavior of many groups throughout history. It also casts something of a positive light on the refugees. We were not fleeing anything as bad as Pharoah, at least not yet, and our percentages were even lower than the ancient Hebrews. But we were and are looking for a better life. ■

22

"ALL MY EXES LIVE IN TEXAS"

"Three chords and the truth" is the accepted prescription for the ideal country song. I learned that probably my second week in the South, and it made a lot of sense when I thought of all the great country musicians this city boy had loved—Hank Williams, Loretta Lynn, and so forth. Simple lyrics. Great voices. The truth...or sort of. Let's say the symbolic truth.

One of my favorite country songs for this reason is George Strait's "All My Exes Live in Texas," its witty lyrics written by Whitey and Linda Shafer. My own exes live in California—but who's counting?

The first place I thought about leaving the Golden State for was Texas. I had once been invited to the state by its then-governor, Rick Perry, who was a fan of new media figures such as, unsurprisingly, the late Andrew Breitbart and, more surprisingly, me. The occasion was to go target shooting with the governor. It gave me my first opportunity in years to take a close look at the state. The few times before I had been racing through the Panhandle at a breakneck pace on my way back and forth between the coasts. I saw little more than dead armadillos splayed on asphalt.

The first thing to surprise me as I got into a rental car at the Austin airport was how much better shape the highways were in than the Los Angeles freeways I had just left. In Southern California they only looked perfect around Disneyland. Here, they were immaculate practically everywhere. How could that possibly be when Texas had no state income tax? Who was paying for the roads?

That was more than a decade ago. I went back to Texas a couple of times thereafter, once to join the governor at the Texas Motor Freeway, where I learned, as Perry announced to an adoring crowd, that "Texans love their guns and NASCAR!"

As I said, that was a while ago. Now even NASCAR is banning some gun advertising, and Austin has long since turned into an outpost of West Los Angeles, vying for the "Most Woke" city in the country award. Refugees from California were certainly still coming to Austin, but it was a different crowd, for whom migration was more like a distinction without a difference.

But my third trip to Texas, in December 2015, was more in the tradition of the Lone Star State we know from John Ford movies. I was travelling to be a speaker at the Bullets & Bourbon conference held at the luxury western-style Rough Creek Lodge, just over an hour's drive from Dallas/Fort Worth Airport. That was the Texas of legend, only real—wide-open spaces as far as the eye could see. It was also, alas, the place where Chris Kyle, the Navy SEAL hero memorialized by Clint Eastwood's *American Sniper*, was shot in cold blood by Marine veteran Eddie Routh, a man Kyle was trying to help work through post-traumatic stress disorder.

This happened on the same range where the other speakers and I were trying our luck with weapons we had never used, and in my case never seen. It was a range the scale of which I had also never seen—very Texan, you might say—where the targets were so far off you couldn't even see them with the telescopic lens on the rifle. I had no real idea where I was shooting, as dust puffed up in barely visible spurts from the hills that seemed to be miles off. I had no future as a sniper.

We were there at the behest of my friends Ed Driscoll and Nina

Yablok, who were the first acquaintances of mine, and really the first people I knew of, who fled blue California for a new life in a red state.

They had been residents of San Jose who visited Texas frequently, loved it, and bought a place in the state, thinking they would retire there. California becoming increasingly miserable, they retired earlier than planned by a number of years, moving to their home near Glen Rose, Texas, in March 2015. In that sense the Rough Creek Lodge event was their coming-out party as newly christened Texans. They had invited their old friends from media outlets like PJ Media and *National Review*, a lineup of conservative pundits including Glenn Reynolds, Dana Loesch, Ed Morrissey, Kevin D. Williamson, and Stephen Green. Perhaps Driscoll (himself a conservative commentator) and Yablok wanted not to feel lonely in their new home. Or maybe they wanted us to feel jealous of where they had gone.

In late 2022, I talked with Nina, a business lawyer who had worked for PJ Media when I was CEO and whom I had known since the early days of the blogosphere around 2003. I asked how she was faring after years living in Texas and what she thought about the move.

"There isn't a day that doesn't pass that we aren't really, really happy that we moved," she said. "We're happy we're not in California, but more so we love Texas."

"Well, tell me about Texas, and how and why your love for Texas has grown."

Nina didn't answer that one directly; instead she told me about a woman she obviously disdained who also moved to Texas from California, but only for the cheap housing and jobs. This woman didn't really know Texas, in Nina's view. Another transplanted "city girl" she criticized was one who couldn't handle the amount of wildlife that normally lives outside but would come indoors during the cold winter, like the occasional gecko.

Texas appealed to Nina because of its Judeo-Christian ethic and the manners still prevalent in the small towns of the state. These were churchgoing people, and, although Nina was Jewish, she appreciated that. She recalled a nine-year-old boy who was among some families touring a new restaurant and who ran forward, unbidden, politely to hold first one door and then another for the adults. In general, if you said something to a child in their part of Texas, the child would engage, looking you in the eye, unlike in California, where children would usually turn away, unwilling or afraid to connect with adults. I knew what she meant.

From what were now seven years of experience, she isolated two kinds of California refugees. Those looking only for cheaper houses with more space tended to move to Washington or Oregon— California lite, in essence. Those motivated by ideology came to Texas, her part anyway. Those were the only ones she saw near her. She would assume newcomers were that way until they showed themselves to be otherwise. And few did.

I was impressed, but not surprised, how Nina and, by extension, Ed were at peace with their environment. How it had become home. Nina, the only Jew for miles, enjoyed giving annual seders for gentiles who had never been to one before. They loved it, she said.

And although Texas was home to many contrary forces, Nina and Ed didn't feel the need to make it perfect the way many of the refugees did, including Sheryl and me back in Tennessee. The couple weren't heavily involved in local politics, nor did they feel compelled to be so. This is not to say they weren't aware of and naturally irritated by the likes of perpetual candidate Beto O'Rourke, parading about the state urging the confiscation of assault weapons, even though he was hard put to define what they were. They were content to let Texas be Texas with all its pluses and minuses, as long as their little bit of heaven was what it was. It wasn't so small anyway. Nothing in Texas was. And they didn't even care that the state's offshore water was, in Nina's words, pretty muddy by comparison with California and elsewhere when they flew down to Houston to join a cruise, their preferred vacation method.

Their confidence in Texas had much to do with a lengthy period of preparation and research. The couple had planned their migration for years, making many trips to the state, becoming, in a sense, habitués, before they made the formal move. It wasn't a sudden lurch, as it had been for so many others. They had made the move mentally before arriving physically. What's more, Ed had been building his recording studio outside the house so it could be operational in advance of move-in day. He also appeared regularly on Glenn Reynolds's InstaPundit, documenting the affairs of the day. Some of these appearances involved Texas, as when Governor Greg Abbott gained much credit among local conservatives for instigating the shipment of illegal immigrants to New York and Washington, to the consternation of those blue cities' mayors.

What you believe about your new location may be more important than the location itself. Texas is a mythical place, just as is California.

One of the questions potential California expats frequently ask existing California expats is whether they can get good sushi in their new home. California, many thought, had the best sushi outside Japan. Even some Japanese I knew agreed, although perhaps they were being polite, as the Japanese are known to be. Nevertheless, Nina insisted there was excellent sushi in a town twenty minutes away from her rural Texas home. I wondered. It was hard to believe the sushi was decent, so far from the ocean in places with such a small clientele. I guess it depended on your definition of "good sushi," but if you were happy with it, then you were happy with it.

One of the keys to living contentedly as a refugee is to accept the reality and lifestyle of your new home. Texas, like California, had multiple lifestyles. Therefore, there are many different ones to consider and accept. Few American refugees went to the treacherous border. They had seen enough on television. The cities, too, were mostly blue. Those who chose a rural life somewhere in the middle of the giant state, like Ed and Nina, had an easier time.

In fact, it was easier for Nina and Ed than any I had met in any of the red states. They are a childless older couple and were able to avoid the treachery of the schools that often provided a catch-22 for migrants. Their internet-dependent careers, too, were largely unaffected by the move, nor did COVID threaten to close them down and disrupt their new lives before they started, as it did so many small business owners looking to restart in new locations.

Ed and Nina's adaptation to Texas was nothing but admirable and could even be an inspiration to others, even as we live through an increasingly dark period, the country continuing to divide, the states themselves dividing between blue cities and red countryside. Indeed, things had become even bleaker as I was writing this book, even more divided. People were being tripped up, right and left.

Life wasn't that simple. Take the example of California migrant Todd Homme and his wife, Tonya. On the surface, these two would have seemed to be as prepared as Ed and Nina. The Hommes had done their research, and they had considerable résumés to bring with them. She was a credentialed Spanish teacher. What skill could be more transferrable to Texas? But Todd's résumé was somewhat more fraught. A well-trained and experienced musician, he had spent much of his life working in various musical capacities for Disney. ∎

23

CAN YOU "WISH UPON A STAR" ANYMORE?

As almost everyone knows, the Walt Disney Company is a powerful presence in California and Florida, as well as in Shanghai, Paris, and many other places across the globe. The company influences the minds of humanity's young at their most impressionable ages as virtually no other institution has, although recently the Chinese Communist Party's social media giant TikTok has given Disney serious competition.

Disney's value system was traditional and patriotic for many years after its founding in 1923. But it has taken a radical change in recent years, veering to the world of woke. Disney had joined the ESG pack. In fact, it was leading it. The old Disney—that of Jiminy Cricket, who urged us to wish upon that star and kept us on the straight and narrow—was vanishing, or at least the nature of those iconic personalities was making a dramatic change. Rumors of some of the darkest corners of human personality—child molestation— had surfaced concerning the employees, even at the executive level.

Recently, however, Disney has taken something of a course correction, rehiring former CEO Bob Iger in response to shareholders who were dismayed by the wokeness and the attendant rebellion of patrons. At the end of 2022 Disney had its worst stock performance in fifty years. Nevertheless, more than a trace of wokeness remains in many corners of the company. Despite Iger, the cultural mood of Disney, and that of Hollywood at large, has not changed at all.

I worked for Disney myself twice as a screenwriter in the late eighties, during the Michael Eisner/Jeffrey Katzenberg regime, on two movies that were made (the successful one by another studio), but I never dreamed that the company would turn the way it has, despite its having been sarcastically nicknamed "Mouseschwitz" by some of its employees. And a mighty turn this was. At that juncture, it was arguably the most powerful media company on the planet.

At a certain point, working for a culturally malignant organization becomes untenable, as it did for Todd Homme. Homme had for decades been a music executive and consultant for Disney, DreamWorks (originally distributed by Disney), and Imagineering (part of Disney), but he left Los Angeles for Franklin, Tennessee, in 2018. To paraphrase the 1976 movie *Network*, he may not have been exactly "mad as hell," but he certainly couldn't "take it anymore." If he was going to keep working for Hollywood, which he did to some extent, he was going to do it as far as possible from Burbank, California, and in a healthier environment. The Seven Dwarfs designed by architect Michael Graves for the postmodern facade of Disney Studios were no longer for Todd. But moving his family was a slow and difficult process, as it was for many. The Hommes didn't just pack up and go.

Nevertheless, as devout Christians, he and his younger wife Tonya were highly disturbed by the uber-woke Los Angeles school systems—public, private, and parochial. They had a daughter in middle school, and her future looked bleak, with years of forced indoctrination ahead. Tonya was a Spanish teacher who worked in Chicago schools and for ten years in Los Angeles. She had observed the process up close in the blue states. It wasn't hard to see where it was going.

Metro Nashville seemed like a good place for the Hommes; Todd was in the music business and had worked there briefly during the eighties. He didn't have to give up everything in moving to that part of Tennessee. And his wife could teach. Schools were always looking for qualified teachers, especially in foreign languages. Finding the right location was a question of research online and in-person trips. They did this assiduously. Schools were paramount in their selection. They were doing this primarily for their daughter. They could have stayed in LA for their careers, living far from the decay of Los Angeles in a clean suburb only a mile from the Kardashians.

From that research, they discovered what many others had: that Williamson County in Tennessee had what was reputed to be one of the best public educational systems in the country. They bought a house there. At that point, Todd told me, he felt like a hero, having put aside his own needs for the benefit of his family.

But trouble began to arise soon after their move. Todd was able to pursue his music business work with Disney and others from afar (fitfully anyway), but Tonya, who had obtained a job teaching Spanish in a local school, ran into difficulties. A war was on in the community not only over curricula, as we have seen, but also over COVID restrictions. The two conflicts seemed to run in tandem, the enforcement of so-called progressive curricula buttressed by the medical restrictions on the part of the entrenched authorities. Tonya, teaching a foreign language, was more or less free from progressive curriculum intrusions, but she didn't want to obey those COVID decrees, particularly the mandatory wearing of masks, which she felt rendered learning her subject impossible, notably the pronunciation of foreign words.

Over a long lunch, Todd had a lot to say about what transpired:

It went like this. The kids got situated at the appropriate distance and then she was okay with that. Then Tonya would remove her mask to begin the lessons of how to learn these new words and these new vowel sounds so they could actually learn something. Well, long story short, some of the other teachers on the hall ratted her out. She was spied out a couple of times where people would drop by to say hi, but they were really just getting a vision of her without a mask on.

And then on one fateful day, they told her she needed to wear a mask. "What if I don't?" "Well, if you don't, then I better tell the principal." So then the vice principal comes by, but Tonya's a bit of a cool customer. She was sitting on the desk. "I have a life," she said. "I'm not wearing this." So they call the principal out of a meeting and he writes her up sitting there, and she was suspended without pay. And so it would be for essentially ten months. And she languished, wondering what's going to happen, and finally there was a Zoom trial with Jason Golden, the head of the school district.

The story—as Todd told it, and I believed him—sounded like Kafka come to Williamson County. The complicated legal process ended with a hearing by a judge "rented" by the county to show impartiality.

As Todd recounted, "Anyway, the rental judge now has, I think, two weeks or something like that to render an opinion, and he writes a twelve-page opinion of the four-hour procedure. And, of course, he finds that she was insubordinate. That was what the charge was. It wasn't about COVID at all. It was about insubordination. And then he admits, 'Of course these masks are not much more than a third-grade arts and crafts project, that we do there to comfort the parents.'"

The Hommes moved from California to "free Tennessee" for this? ■

24

SAVED BY A PUCK

Yet the Hommes are still here. Their daughter, having had predictable difficulties in the Williamson system, is now being homeschooled, as are many who have undergone similar experiences. Meanwhile, homeschooling in the area had been formalized and advanced considerably. Consequently, the curriculum had become far more challenging—and educationally productive—than the public and most other local schools. Latin was mandatory as a basis. They instituted a serious reading list that was similar to the old University of Chicago Great Books for Kids Program (1962), in which *Adventures of Huckleberry Finn* was still required and not canceled for supposed racism and more difficult works like *The Pilgrim's Progress* were also mandatory.

There have been dropouts from this rigorous program, but not the Hommes' daughter. She came from parents who are smart and educated, which sometimes can be a detriment when making the move across the country, especially for the parents themselves. Though you don't want to, you retain a kind of snobbery. You may have come from a certain coastal tradition. You may have gone to an Ivy League school or schools that, although they have become heavily corrupted in the woke era and you may no longer donate as an alumnus, retain a certain cachet for yourself and others. This is true to an extent in the South as well, as that same superiority (earned or not, as these institutions have gone woke as well) is attached to the University of the South (Sewanee) and to Vanderbilt and Duke, which have approached near-Ivy status.

I shared this problem, this duality, with Todd Homme. Neither of us wanted to believe we had come to the land of the yahoos, but sometimes we did. In my case, I sometimes also felt I was that other paradigm, the city slicker gulled by the country bumpkins.

But we both, by habit, looked below the surface. Todd, a Canadian by birth and athletic for a man in his sixties, had taken to playing regular amateur hockey to maintain that fitness and to remind him of home. He admitted he was having trouble adjusting to Tennessee. He used to play as a youth in Canada and continued in Los Angeles, where the game was popular with certain Hollywood types. So he picked it up again in Tennessee and discovered something in the process. Other players, many of whom were also from California and who came from various social and economic classes, were having similar problems. He could see it in their eyes at those hockey games, which took place in different rinks across the Metro Nashville area. These men were feeling disconnected and without purpose after a few years. It was easy to understand. Back home, wherever that had been, they had respectable jobs that connected them to their communities and supported their families. In Tennessee it was not so easy, and they were not of retirement age. It was even harder for those who had been in positions of authority before, but who had to start over, middle-aged, in their new home.

These men were told from childhood that their work defined them. With their new, unfulfilling careers, what was left? Many played hockey to fill the void. But was that enough?

For me, there was a better answer than hockey. It was tennis. And I was the sole migrant in the game. But more on that later. ∎

25

COULD "THE FARMER AND THE COWMAN" BE FRIENDS?

A s you age and the hard drive that is your brain fills up, there tends to be less room for current popular entertainment—movies, plays, art, especially music. (That's the number one hit? Oh, really.) You often feel out of the loop, and you wonder what else you are missing. If you are like me, you try to keep up, because you don't want to feel out of it. Politics, as Andrew Breitbart said long ago, is "downstream of culture." If Stephen Colbert is the king of late night, maybe there is, after all, something to second graders getting to choose their sex... Well, maybe not.

But in the midst of this ongoing Kulturkampf, images and fragments from a bygone world, a long-ago youth, pop up at odd moments. Recently, the lyrics of a number from Rodgers and Hammerstein's *Oklahoma!* (which debuted on Broadway eight months before I was born and which reached the screen when I was barely eleven) were going through my head like a jukebox on replay—as I tried to fall asleep at night, as I brushed my teeth in the morning.

It wasn't one of the great classics from the musical, like "Oh, What a Beautiful Mornin'" and "People Will Say We're in Love." It was "The Farmer and the Cowman," a dance number. Why this one? I wondered. What was my unconscious trying to tell me? It was repeating in the way that memories invade our dreams.

Maybe this had bubbled up because it was a time of increasing violence in our country not seen in decades, here in Tennessee but virtually everywhere, particularly in our cities. Around the same time, a nineteen-year-old in Memphis, who had been recently indicted for attempted murder and who should have been incarcerated for a decade but who was out in eleven months, went on a murder rampage, including killing a woman in front of her daughter.

That song—that endorsed friendship between the normally oppositional cowboys and farmers for the benefit of all—had been playing in my mind for several weeks before this event. Something else had generated it. I solved the mystery when I sat down for lunch with Jack Johnson, the state senator and powerful majority leader many were talking about as the next governor. We had last met on talk radio nearly four years before, and I assumed we were in many ways political adversaries. He was the personification of the Tennessee Republican establishment, and I the personification of the California interloper about whom Jack had shown such frustration, as you will recall from his conversations with Galen Walker of the Bold Patriot Brewery. ("What is it about you Californians?" he had asked Galen. Was Johnson, as Robert De Niro's famous line went in *Taxi Driver*, "talkin' to me?")

Before our lunch, I assumed Johnson would be in a bad mood. He had just barely squeaked out a primary victory (in August 2022) in his Williamson County district that most, including me, thought would be a cake walk. He had a sixteen-year incumbency; oodles of cash; name recognition; the backing of Governor Lee and the state's two U.S. Senators, Marsha Blackburn and Bill Hagerty; and a series of professional television ads highlighting his role in keeping the Tennessee tax rate the lowest in the nation or close. Yet he won by only slightly more than seven hundred votes, roughly 3 percent.

His opponent was Gary Humble, founder of Tennessee Stands and an archetypal refugee/migrant, although he came from Texas, not California. Humble had run a ground game campaign based largely on two issues: the corruption of the schools and election integrity. Tennessee, like virtually everywhere else in the United States, had a wretched school system pervaded with left-wing bias, and this apparently had resonated with a surprising percentage of voters, although the election, like so many state level elections, had had a ridiculously low turnout. This gave the activists, composed to a great extent of Californians—or "Californios," as I privately called them, after the original Spanish colonists of the Golden State—substantial power. These migrant activists came within a whisker of upending Jack. Gary Humble was the newcomer, their brother, to whom they naturally gravitated. I know I did. And besides, Humble was the sexy radical in the modern sense. He was the militant constitutionalist seeking to bring the country back to the ideals of the Founders. (Later, in 2023, these same activists *would* upend the establishment Williamson County Republican Committee.)

Nevertheless, Jack was smiling that day, exuding the casual charm of the experienced politician. His was the kind of personality that makes a tense lunch more pleasant, and I liked him for it. After all, now he would remain in office in an overwhelmingly Republican county. Why shouldn't he be happy? As he explained, he had nothing against the newcomers, and he even admired them and their ideas. But they did not know, he said, the history of the state—of how recently it had turned Republican and of the battles that he and others fought to make it so. There was truth to this.

And yet, all the while, those lyrics by Oscar Hammerstein were playing in my mind. It was becoming evident why my unconscious had glommed on to them, although it wasn't clear to me who were the farmers and who the cowboys.

Maybe it didn't matter. Our country was falling apart. Protestors, accused of being insurrectionists but without real weapons or the slightest means of enacting said insurrection, languished in jails with little hope of a fair trial. An ex-president's private home was invaded by a lawless FBI. Soon enough a pillow entrepreneur who publicly questioned the 2020 election would be surrounded by feds at a Minnesota restaurant, his cell phone confiscated. This had become par for the course. The government was waging a war on conservatives seemingly everywhere. If the farmers and the cowboys couldn't be friends now, what hope did our republic have? As Hammerstein wrote, folks out in the "territory" would be smart to band together. The red states, as far as I could tell, were very much still "the territories," but they were no longer the pristine arcadia of the musical's Oklahoma. The real "territories" had been corrupted for years.

So I asked Jack—gingerly, as I saw no reason to alienate him—if he had learned something from the surprise closeness of the primary vote.

I found it easier to talk with Jack Johnson, in a certain way, than with Gary Humble. Given my Hollywood background and years in publishing, I was more comfortable with establishment people than with the insurgents, although intellectually I was most often aligned with the insurgents. In that way, I embodied the split in the Rodgers and Hammerstein song. "The Farmer and the Cowman" had been written as a cute dance number, but the contemporary state of our nation had given this old tune a new and serious message.

This song embodied the dilemma the refugees had as new arrivals in the "territory." At the same time it contained wisdom for the incumbents, like Jack, who would be well advised to heed the newcomers' complaints in order to facilitate, if it were even possible, what amounted to a return to an older version of America.

But was that old America ever really there? Even Alexis de Tocqueville had complaints—plenty of them actually. The Frenchman, like H. L. Mencken after him, saw Americans as too obsessed with making money.

What we were after, perhaps, was the old America perfected. ■

26

A NEW DEBATE FOR
THE NEW OLD AMERICA

As the brouhaha over Robby Starbuck and Morgan Ortagus died down (it never completely disappeared because Robby was suing the Republican Party SEC for keeping him off the ballot and Morgan was apparently trying to piggyback on his lawsuit), the congressional election in the Tennessee Fifth, which had ballooned into a national cause célèbre, looked to be returning to normal.

For once, my blogger friend Rocky Top had been wrong. He predicted that Robby and Morgan would leave Tennessee. Yet they were hanging around as the elections of November 2022 approached. It was unclear for what reason, other than that suit. Perhaps it was too embarrassing to go back to Southern California and DC, respectively, with their tails between their legs. Or maybe they just liked it here, as many of us do.

Meanwhile, the election in the Tennessee Fifth had devolved into something more conventional, sans carpetbaggers, although a relatively small number of the "cavalry" still supported Robby as a write-in candidate. He was their leader, *faute de mieux*. Sometimes I imagined them all going off into the woods like some band of revolutionaries, waiting for the propitious moment to make their triumphant return. It was somehow appropriate given Robby's quasi-Cuban background, even with the obvious role reversal. He would be the anti-communist *caudillo*. But more likely they were locked in their rooms writing nasty text messages about those of us who thought Morgan and Robby might have been a little presumptuous in their attempts to achieve near-instant political stardom via the citizens of Tennessee.

About this time, my wife, Sheryl Longin, had a spontaneous idea about how to elevate the tawdry level of political debate in our country.

Who could forget the moment when Fox's Chris Wallace squelched Donald Trump's questions about Hunter Biden's laptop during the 2020 presidential debates? "Corrupt" may be too a weak word for Wallace's conduct. "Despicable" might be more accurate.

Sheryl was by then first vice president of the Nashville Republican Women, the longest-lasting and probably most important red activist group in that blue city. In this role, she was in charge of getting speakers for the group. Her relatively rapid elevation in the area probably had something to do with what she and I carried with us from California, and in my case New York as well: an innate competitive urgency—that "New York minute" thing—that was not always present in the heartland.

In one of those late-night casual husband–wife conversations—ours had generally veered to the political over the years—Sheryl proposed doing something different. Instead of journalists, almost all of whom were biased like Wallace, why not have the respective experts of various fields—the economy, immigration, and so forth—ask questions of candidates?

I liked the idea immediately but wondered aloud if anyone would possibly do such a thing. Then I suddenly realized that if someone would do it, I worked for that organization—the *Epoch Times*. They had the ability, television crews, and contacts necessary to bring in the potential experts. I wondered if they would like the idea.

They did. I contacted senior editor Jan Jekielek, who was immediately intrigued. What followed, however, was the bumpy road typical for something that had never been tried before, particularly those events that take place under lights and cameras. Sheryl and I quickly likened staging this debate to the ups and downs of making independent movies, a constantly hair-raising experience we had had before. You never know if your "passion project" will really materialize until you are standing on the set with cameras rolling. Even then, it's touch and go.

We were having a similar problem with our political debate reform, whose intentions couldn't have been more idealistic.

To begin with, when word leaked out what we were planning, the responses were far from wholeheartedly positive. Most, but not all, of the refugees we talked to supported it, but entrenched forces tended to be skeptical. You could call them RINOs, but I suspect that for many, a considerably more enduring human trait was at play—jealousy. We were facing the "it's no good if I'm not doing it" stance. We got a lot of patronizing smiles from these people, the clever among them asking why so-called domain "experts" should be any less biased than reporters.

No one is more biased than reporters, I was tempted to say, though I acknowledged they had a point. I would go on to explain that experts normally have more allegiance to the truth than journalists. Experts depended on being perceived as honest about their fields. It was a professional matter. Well, mostly.

Nevertheless, we knew we had to be very careful about the experts we chose. We left that responsibility, for the most part, in the hands of Jan Jekielek. Jan had met a staggering number of experts in fields from medicine to immigration to economics on his *American Thought Leaders* interview show for Epoch TV. He essentially covered the bases. The motto of the *Epoch Times* was "Truth and Tradition." In my experience, Jan followed it.

That left Sheryl and me to find a venue for the event and to convince the leading candidates in the Fifth Congressional District to participate.

The first item on the to-do list came easily. Indeed, it proved to be something of bonanza, though with strange caveats. The Nashville Republican Women had teamed up with two Young Republican groups—one in Davidson County, contiguous with Nashville, and one in neighboring Williamson—both of which were partly in the newly drawn district, supposedly favorable to the GOP. When we first met them over dinner, it turned out Nathan Green of the Davidson group had already solved that venue problem perfectly, or so it seemed. Though a young man in his twenties, he was already active in state government and had just the right place in mind for us. It was the Mason's Grand Lodge of Tennessee (Nathan was a Mason) that happened to be about a five-minute walk from where we were eating.

So, off we went to the Grand Lodge, a large, austere building built in the neoclassical style in 1925, located just one block south of all the wild honky-tonk tourist activity on Broadway. I had walked past it many times without noticing it, perhaps because of its garish neighbors all bathed in neon, and because I did not know much about the Masons. Nevertheless, within minutes we were being let in through the back door by a friendly Mason. We plowed through a vast, almost industrial kitchen that could have fed an army, or part of one, and continued into the even more vast caverns of the Grand Lodge.

There we were surrounded by walls covered in oil portraits of bearded gentlemen of bygone, more formal eras. On one wall was Andrew Jackson, the nation's seventh president and Tennessee's most renowned historical figure, who was evidently a Mason. Elsewhere one saw a number of other US presidents, from George Washington to Harry Truman and Gerald Ford.

Jackson's portrait, appropriately, was the most prominent. I had visited his home and estate, the Hermitage, slightly north of

Nashville, as an obligatory mission within a few weeks of moving to Tennessee. I knew he was a favorite of Trump's for saving the country as US general in the Battle of New Orleans. I also knew that he is often accused of anti-Indian racism, making him a notoriously controversial figure and another convenient means by which to bash Trump. But I hadn't realized how accessible to the public his lovely home was during his presidency (1829–1837). Hard as it is to comprehend in our era, anyone could just walk up to the door and knock when Jackson was in residency to ask a question of the president. These days most presidents, Joe Biden especially, try to make themselves as scarce as possible. They are surrounded by security every moment. Andrew Jackson was evidently too macho for that. Old Hickory was his own security.

The Masons were all set on the security front. Their Tennessee headquarters was almost a fort. I was impressed, yet I was still apprehensive about using it for the debate because the slightly tarnished decoration and the building itself seemed something from a fading past. I imagined it would have an auditorium space akin to my elementary school, with its hoary wooden desks out of the nineteenth century.

Was I wrong! We emerged in a raked three-quarter-round space that would have been the envy of most Off-Broadway theater companies. It was perfect for our (or any) debate, a veritable Lincoln Center in Nashville. Who knew?

Not very many people, it soon became clear, not just when I talked about it to acquaintances but more ominously when I bragged about the venue publicly, in an article I wrote for the *Epoch Times* promoting the coming debate. A number of irate commenters attacked us viciously for consorting with satanists. Were the Masons satanists? George Washington was a satanist? ("Father, I cannot tell a lie. I am the Devil's spawn...and, by the way, all our cherry trees are poisoned.")

I didn't believe this paranoid nonsense for a second but worried that the false accusation—evidently centuries old—would be used to besmirch our idea for a new kind of debate, which all involved hoped would take hold across the nation as the new standard.

So the group of us barged into the lobby of the Masonic headquarters, confronting its Grand Master, who at first seemed confused as to who we were. We wanted to know if we could use the lodge for our debate. I, and even Sheryl, generally a nicer person than I am, could come off as pushy and aggressive to local Tennesseans, even if they largely agreed with us politically. I realized this is how I appeared just now, and I felt momentarily sheepish.

This benign assertiveness was partly the result of our coming from California and New York. Both places, as I mentioned, installed in its residents a considerably higher degree of push, a kind of onboard motor, endemic to those locales, no matter how you viewed the world or whether you despised what those places had become. That motor was installed anyway. It could be good or bad, depending on where you applied your energy. But you were well advised to keep it from running too hot. It was worth considering that there was something worthwhile to the South's slower-moving culture.

In this case we were able to make friends with the Grand Master, who was especially welcoming after the initial confusion and gave us permission to use the facility. I learned later he was something of a liberal in internal Masonic politics since he favored allowing alcohol on the premises, a longtime prohibition for the society.

With the apparently prearranged approval of the Grand Master, we all agreed the Grand Lodge of Tennessee would be the home of our debate. The price was quite reasonable. We decided the best solution to the problem of the anti-Mason ankle-biters was to ignore them—they were, as far as we could tell, a small group—and to concentrate on the more significant issue of getting the candidates to agree to participate.

Looking back, the whole debate adventure was an amusing though nerve-racking experiment in modern politics. There's a moral to this story, as well as a happy (with limitations) ending for its sponsors.

One of the decisions a candidate makes in any campaign is whether to debate his opponents. This becomes a question of risks and rewards, one that throughout the second half of 2022 was being asked in races across the country, during both primaries and general elections. During the Arizona gubernatorial and the Pennsylvania senatorial elections, where it was unclear whether the Democratic candidate was compos mentis, the debate question itself predominated among major issues.

The various accusations went: so-and-so refused to debate; so-and-so refused to debate until weeks after early voting had already commenced, limiting its impact. For candidates who chose not to debate, unpopular policy stances wouldn't have to be revealed or untangled. All kinds of chicanery could flow from the latter.

Much of this played out in Arizona gubernatorial race, where the feisty Trump-supporting former news anchor Kari Lake kept trying to debate the secretary of state Katie Hobbs, and in the Pennsylvania senatorial contest, where Dr. Mehmet Oz was trying to do the same with his Democratic adversary, John Fetterman, who suffered a serious stroke during the campaign.

Some of this may have been a charade, of course. It was unclear if any of the above candidates really wanted to debate. They only wanted to demonstrate to supporters that their opponent was afraid to do so. The ultimate losers in these media-spurred catfights were the voters.

Earlier, the Tennessee Fifth had presented similar challenges that we wanted to avoid. We were doing this to educate the voters in ways that had never been tried before.

As mentioned, the district had been redrawn by a Republican legislature. The new Fifth spanned six counties that favored the GOP overall. Some of blue Davidson (Nashville) remained in the district, but five other overwhelmingly red counties—Wilson,

Williamson, Maury, Marshall, and Lewis, the latter three in their entirety—were added to ensure Republican victories.

Because of this redistricting, there was no incumbent. This meant the number of people who registered interest in the position was initially staggering, even with Robby Starbuck and Morgan Ortagus officially out. That interest eventually started to recede—some of the wannabes realizing their dreams of Capitol Hill glory might actually cost them money—but it still stood at nine candidates, too many for a serious debate, when we began to organize ours.

Consulting what sketchy polls there were, and with a little help from our Young Republican colleagues Stevie Giorno and Nathan Green, plus advice from various politicos about town, we winnowed our list down to the candidates who had a chance. Those politicos identified only three who they said "really had a chance":

Beth Harwell—the first woman Speaker of the Tennessee House and currently on the board of directors of the Tennessee Valley Authority. Harwell, although she lost in the most recent gubernatorial contest to Bill Lee, was considered the front-runner.

Andy Ogles—the conservative activist mayor of Maury County (Columbia) who had opposed COVID vaccine mandates in his county. He was backed by the Koch brothers' Americans for Prosperity and had made previous attempts for higher office, including the GOP nomination for the US Senate when the old guard Republican Bob Corker was in office.

Kurt Winstead—the previously mentioned retired National Guard brigadier general.

I knew both Harwell and Ogles. Harwell was a near neighbor. Some mutual friends once invited us to have dinner with her, and I also saw her at other various local events. I joined Ogles several times on Michael Patrick Leahy's *Tennessee Star Report*. I liked both candidates.

I had no such personal knowledge of the third favorite, Brigadier General Kurt Winstead, except that he supposedly had a great deal of money he was willing to put into the campaign. Most of these funds came from his wife, who, to my astonishment, was a Democratic Party lobbyist with close ties to Big Pharma and Big Tech. Winstead later explained that he and his wife did not share the same politics. Not everybody was buying it. In fact, it was hard to determine what Winstead's politics actually were.

Of those leading candidates, Ogles agreed to debate immediately. Harwell, however, equivocated. She gave repeated excuses that didn't add up: fundraisers in DC that didn't sound exactly like fundraisers, vague meetings that always were on the day of the debate. Admittedly, we changed the day once to accommodate the *Epoch Times*, which was using the same crew for the Freedom Fest in Las Vegas, but she knew of this change long in advance.

We spent a good deal of time wooing Harwell, sometimes directly and sometimes through a mutual friend who was urging her to participate. It never worked. Once she mumbled to me that Ogles was such a good debater and knew the issues well. She sounded afraid, though I had heard Harwell speak intelligently about the issues when she gave a fluent talk to the Nashville Republican Women. She also taught government at Middle Tennessee State University.

This was odd behavior for a former Speaker. Rocky Top had warned me of this. With his typical snark, he called Harwell a member of the "Bathroom Caucus," describing how she would disappear into the ladies' room in the lead-up to an important vote until she knew which way the political wind was blowing. I had no way of corroborating that.

I smelled another reason she was holding back. She had hired a powerful Beltway political consulting firm—TLC Political— undoubtedly for a pretty penny. These sorts of consultants don't come cheap. TLC's chief strategist (that word should take scare quotes) served as the national political director for former Speaker Paul Ryan's PAC. Another company executive led multiple Republican senatorial campaigns. When you pay that kind of money, you tend to feel you must heed their advice. They told her she was the front-runner, and that she could only lose by debating. Of course, they were totally wrong in that regard, not that anyone would notice. Such is the way of those firms. They take the money and run, and Harwell should have known better. Maybe Rocky Top was right, that Harwell was merely hiding from conflict behind a shield of fancy consultants. Whatever the case, it left us with a gaping hole in our debate.

We did, however, have Kurt Winstead and his well-heeled campaign. Or so we thought. He had given us his personal assurances. But as we drew close to the day, the brigadier general suddenly went radio silent. Apparently his (less glamorous) consultants were giving him the same advice—don't debate—but for a better reason than Harwell's. Winstead, who had appeared on several local talk radio shows, was a terrible candidate whose knowledge of the issues was remarkably shallow—embarrassingly so. He hid behind pandering television commercials—the "I'm just a good old country boy like you" variety—that were insultingly devoid of content. He was also, in our experience, a liar.

A Debate without Candidates?

So, a day or two before the debate, we didn't have two of the three leading candidates. We worried that no audience would show up—or, worse still, that no one would watch the debate on Epoch TV, which was broadcasting it over the internet, something that had never been done for a congressional election, primary or not.

We further worried that our experts would drop out. We had already lost Dr. Wilfred Reilly, an associate political science professor from Kentucky State, in the education area and had to replace him at the last minute with Dr. Carol Swain. Swain's bootstrapped personal history, from abject poverty as one of twelve children living in a shack with no running water to professorships at Princeton and Vanderbilt, is extraordinary. She was nobody's idea of a second choice, and would normally have been our first, but we had initially wanted to avoid local Nashville residents to give the event more of a national veneer. She had also run, unfortunately unsuccessfully, for mayor of the city.

None of that really mattered, though our last-minute rehearsal—conducted roughly a half hour before the event with hundreds of people milling about on the sidewalk in front of the building, waiting to get in—was something of a disorganized, unmitigated disaster. Humiliation awaited.

As often happens in those cases, the actual event went off well. Our experts—economist Jeffrey Tucker, nationally recognized China maven Gordon Chang, election attorney Hans von Spakovsky, and Swain—performed admirably, as did the three candidates, especially Ogles and dark horse Jeff Beierlein, who has a future in politics, should he choose one.

More than five hundred people attended in person, including a number of the refugees, and an astonishing—for a local primary election—51,000 watched the Epoch TV broadcast across the country. These record numbers were all the more surprising because, as it turned out, only a total of about 57,000 people voted in the election. Ogles won the straw poll that night, easily outpolling runners-up Harwell and Winstead. He followed that up with a win in the primary a few months later.

He also easily won the general election against his Democratic opponent and is now an active member of the House Freedom Caucus, although some had predicted he would be a passive backbencher in the end. Evidently not. Even before being sworn in, he was one of only thirteen brave House Republicans to sign a letter to his Senate colleagues warning them against signing the huge ($1.7 trillion, as it turned out) omnibus spending bill before the end of the year. The letter read, in part, "We are obliged to inform you that if any omnibus passes…we will oppose and whip opposition to any legislative priority of those senators who vote for this bill—including the Republican leader."

As Rocky Top, a friend of Ogles, wrote me in a text, "Andy is taking some chances." Indeed he was. The bill passed with eighteen Republican senators, including Minority Leader Mitch McConnell, voting in favor of the inflationary boondoggle. Despite his trademark snark, I suspect Rocky was proud of Andy.

The freshman congressman also distinguished himself as a prominent member of the twenty who, by withholding approval for a time of Kevin McCarthy's speakership, were able to get the House rules rewritten in a constitutional manner that gladdened the hearts of most of us refugees.

So was our unique debate what launched Ogles's Capitol Hill career? We'd like to think so. At the least it highlighted the fact that his leading adversaries were afraid to debate the issues. (For the record, I would have gladly voted for Harwell in the general, had she won. I'm not so sure about Winstead.) ∎

27

BEWARE THE IDES OF REFUGEE MARCH

Nothing is as good or as bad as it seems. In March 2023 the reputation of our debate winner, now Congressman Andy Ogles, took a serious blow from left-wing journalist Phil Williams of Nashville's News Channel 5. The noxious Williams, normally quick to smear any conservative unfairly, was, in this instance, at least partly on target.

At first, he accused Ogles of résumé padding. The congressman claimed to have a college degree in economics when he actually majored in liberal studies, whatever that is. He also touted a special graduate program in business at Dartmouth when it was really just a brief online survey given by the Ivy League college and open to the public. Other reports of Ogles's exaggerations swirled around.

Although this sort of padding is not exactly a capital offense and is probably practiced by a fair number of politicians, Ogles's responses were shifty and augured more revelations ahead.

There were. Williams, writing at newschannel5.com, revived an old but not easily overlooked story: "Ogles used photo of stillborn child for GoFundMe, promising a place for burial of babies with benches for families, life-size statue of Jesus. It never happened, and he won't say where money went."

The money in question was $25,000. Ogles later said he distributed the cash to the other grieving families, but he couldn't recall who they were or even where they came from. The exonerating fact—that the stillborn child was Andy and his wife's own—was buried by Williams in one of the lowest paragraphs. Nevertheless, the optics, as they say in the political world, were not good.

The scandal spread nationally, to the *Washington Post* among other publications. Ogles is now in the crosshairs for a primary that is less than two years off. His best chance of surviving may be if enough competitors, smelling blood, get into the race, leaving him with some core base.

And this wasn't the only recent Republican disgrace to suddenly materialize that same month. Yet another scandal depressed the refugee population, making us wonder why we came here in the first place. Call it the Ides of Refugee March.

Lieutenant Governor Randy McNally—an aging (seventy-nine-year-old) and supposedly straitlaced crusader for family values—got caught hitting the Instagram "like" button and making suggestive comments on the posts of a half-naked twenty-year-old gay model. Unearthed by the progressive website the Tennessee Holler, these online hypocrisies were simultaneously nauseating and pathetic. Even more nauseating and pathetic was the Republican state senate, which in an overwhelming vote refused to force the lieutenant governor to resign.

A silver lining for supporters of Ogles was that this scandal blew his own off the front pages. Also for fans of the freshman congressman—and I remain one—he honored his campaign pledge by introducing articles of impeachment for Joe Biden and Kamala Harris. ∎

28

FLORIDA—DREAMLAND
OR GRAVE?

After you move to Tennessee, when you wake up one February morning, it's eighteen degrees, and the roads have been covered with black ice for a week, you wonder, "Why in God's name didn't I move to Florida when I had the chance?"

You also might be checking the weather report back in LA and find it is seventy-two and clear, the smog having vanished years ago.

But life isn't about the weather—or is it?

When you live in a Southern state like Tennessee and even Texas, you feel a proximity to Florida that didn't exist in California, New York, Illinois, or certainly Washington State, although in some cases the effective difference is barely more than an hour by plane.

You can drive to northern Florida, and many do, in seven hours to an area once known as the Redneck Riviera (which is also the name of a bourbon made by country star John Rich). When you arrive, you find it is not so "redneck" anymore, in the cliché sense of that term anyway. There are beachfront homes selling for many millions, though even these are not quite as expensive as the mansions of Malibu and the Hamptons. The area is known as the "30A" for a road that runs east to west not far from the beach at the extreme north end of the Gulf of Mexico. Its spotless white-sand beaches are themselves arguably more beautiful than any in Long Island, and its azure waters warmer than those on the East or West Coasts.

I had never heard of this place when I lived in Los Angeles. After I first went there, a friend told me that I was now officially a Nashvillian because I had vacationed on the 30A. I had been to different parts of Florida several times, the first over five decades earlier when I was in graduate school and drove down from New Haven with my then-wife to visit her grandfather, who lived in Miami. I was introduced to the world of the "winkels," Yiddish for corners, where old socialists congregated daily to rehash the never-ending battles between Mensheviks and Bolsheviks.

So my idea of Florida in those days was a place that old Jews— not all of them socialists, obviously—went to die. Many (including that grandfather) physically resembled Mafia financial wizard Meyer Lansky as portrayed by an aging, frail Lee Strasberg in *The Godfather*, and lived in similar one-story pastel-hued residences to avoid having to walk up stairs.

My own parents had a vacation condominium in West Palm Beach, and I wondered if that was where they would ultimately retire, but that was not to be. Still, some of my fondest memories of my father were going with him to view the manatees lurking by local effluences to keep warm. So I had my impressions of Florida over the years, a kind of vacation paradise replete with crocodiles and flamingos but too hot in the summer to consider living there. And then there was *Miami Vice*, making it seem like a playland for arrested adolescents, a little overbearing after the first day or two. Disney World didn't appeal either after your kids reached a certain age. In fact, it had other more serious problems. And who wanted to deal with hurricanes every other year?

But political winds, brought on by COVID and then the Biden administration, shifted, and Florida started to look like a true paradise. Indeed, Florida became the land of the free, the lone true bastion against an overweening federal government. It was a place where kids actually went to school to learn and socialize, whereas in other states students were trapped in their bedrooms with nothing but laptops and cell phones to keep them company. Other states tried to do something about this, but none did as much as Florida. It was a completely different place from the rest of locked-down America.

As Promised, a Second (Very Witty) Markowicz

One prominent person who picked up and moved hearth and home, rather publicly, to the Sunshine State was *New York Post* columnist Karol Markowicz, a longtime Brooklynite. A year after decamping south she demonstrated absolutely no regret for her "betrayal" of Gotham, writing on Fox News: "It wasn't the virus that killed our New York dream. It was the political reaction to that virus. The George Floyd riots in the summer of 2020 shook us but not nearly as much as the response from public health officials saying the protests were OK, or the politicians covering for the destruction of cities across the country with woke platitudes."

Markowicz had it on the button. Our cities were being destroyed, and what she called "woke platitudes" contributed more than their share to this destruction and desecration that was undermining our lives and, more importantly, those of our children. "Platitudes" might even have been an understatement. Covert yet deliberate attacks on free speech and freedom itself could be just as accurate a characterization of the woke ideology. Whatever the case, Markowicz had had enough. As she wrote, "My husband and I sat on a Long Island beach that summer of 2020 and said words we could never have imagined: We've got to go. We have to get our children out of this."

I had the pleasure of talking with Markowicz—whom I knew years ago during the early days of Pajamas Media as Karol Sheinin— on Zoom during the writing of this book. She underscored how important the protection of her children was in motivating her family's move. She and her husband would likely have remained in Brooklyn, she said, had it not been for what they observed happening to their youngest son in kindergarten, where he was forced to wear a mask while being confronted by a masked teacher. Not surprisingly, he was having developmental issues that thankfully vanished rather rapidly when they relocated to Florida. What happened to children during the pandemic is arguably close to the greatest example of mass child abuse ever, and Markowicz has written about it in a new book, *Stolen Youth*. It is notable that the schooling of their children is also what motivated the other Markowiczes, Dave and his wife Tally, to make the move from California to Tennessee.

What surprised Karol during our chat was my description of the fitful conflict here in Tennessee between the sometimes ultra-conservative/libertarian refugees from blue states and the GOP establishment. They don't experience any of that in Florida, which she described as the land of the free.

I recall feeling it was just that as I stepped off a plane in Orlando on the way to a 2021 conference, CPAC, my first visit to the state in some time. It was almost as if I were in another country—or back in the one I recalled only dimly, despite it not having been all that long since Drs. Anthony Fauci and Deborah Birx had so intruded on our lives with their ever-changing draconian decrees. And Orlando, filled with amusement parks but landlocked and without a beach, was far from my favorite part of Florida.

Yet it was surreal and oddly buoyant at that point to see the public—at least a good portion of it—walking about without masks, so accustomed was I to everyone complying with new regulations even in Nashville, where only a few of us early on resisted the massive pressure. Even most of the refugees there were wearing face coverings, although they often apologized for it, making sure you knew they were really opposed.

What gave me that feeling of freedom in Florida, and still does, ultimately came from the presence and actions of one man, Governor Ron DeSantis, who, after an initial wobble, quite early and against much supposedly "scientific" advice had decreed there would be no lockdowns in his state.

Through that he became the most significant governor in memory, having almost single-handedly brought back the concept of federalism conceived by the Founders, a "power to the people" that was realer than the bogus version we knew in the sixties.

He made Florida what he called an "oasis of freedom." I returned from that CPAC wearing a baseball hat emblazoned with a swordfish and reading "Florida DeSantisland." The governor's approval kept growing into the 2022 election, when it became clear that what we were told by federal authorities was "the science" was anything but—if we hadn't intuited it before or read the many available articles from dissenting doctors, a fair number of whom had credentials equal to or even superior to Fauci's.

So when DeSantis walked on stage with his family during a Lynyrd Skynyrd rock concert in Hollywood, Florida, in mid-October 2022, the audience went wild with chants of "USA! USA!" Conservatism was cool, not liberalism and progressivism.

The lead singer of Lynyrd Skynyrd, Johnny Van Zant, and his brother Donny, had already released a song in honor of the governor, "Sweet Florida."

Of course, that was DeSantis's conservatism—there are obviously many—and, as they say, that was then, this is now. And the reality of the now is that the new populist Republican Party belongs, as it did before, to Donald J. Trump, at least as of this writing. Waiting in the wings is a young man named Vivek Ramaswamy, a biotech entrepreneur who has been running a compelling presidential campaign taking Trump's principles further, and simultaneously outdoing DeSantis, whose own presidential campaign, as of May 2023, seems to be stalled. Some major backers were even reneging on their pledges, apparently disturbed by a mishandling of the conflict with Disney.

Nevertheless, to give the Florida governor his due, his state has made dramatic legislative progress. With the backing of a GOP-majority legislature, Ron DeSantis was largely responsible. Once a purple state with legions of lawyers poring over "hanging chads," as they did in the Bush vs. Gore election of 2000, Florida has become solidly red due to the influx of migrants from blue states "yearning to breathe free."

"Give me your tired, your poor," Emma Lazarus famously wrote in her sonnet "The New Colossus," enshrined on the Statue of Liberty. "Your huddle masses yearning to breathe free."

It may seem odd or overblown to use these words to describe our internal refugees. Migrants from California and New York did not come from impoverished banana republics or communist dictatorships out of *Darkness at Noon*. But they were afraid that their own beloved country was turning, in character, into a bizarre combination of all these places.

So come they did, to Florida, Tennessee, Texas, and also to Idaho, Montana, Nevada, South Dakota, and other states less prominent for these migrations. But it was Florida, America's vacationland, that had a state government completely in sync with their desires and motives. Everybody fit right in. Florida was very much the new "golden door" of Lazarus's poem. ("I lift my lamp beside the golden door!") All they had to do was unload the U-Haul and get a new license plate for their car.

Sarasota had become one of the prime destinations for these migrants. Many times when I talked with people back in New York or LA, they would ask me first about Sarasota (The second place? Franklin, Tennessee) as if I were an expert on that part of Florida. I wasn't, although I had passed through, visiting the John and Mable Ringling Museum of Art, with its detailed miniatures of the mobile Barnum & Bailey circuses that once toured the country. After Hurricane Ian, the attraction seemed to wane, but not for long. Electricity was back in nearly all of Florida in ten days, DeSantis, an organized man, announced. The freedom rush would begin again soon.

At the same time, sides were quietly being chosen on the right for the contest between Trump and DeSantis for the next Republican presidential nomination. Or maybe not so quietly. This was going on among the refugees even before the midterm elections. The prospect that the GOP might take over the House and Senate only intensified this competition. The general atmosphere for Republicans had become so positive—the expectation of a "Red Wave" so pervasive, as reflected in polls by Trafalgar and others— that I was beginning to think this book would become irrelevant before I had finished it. The blue-to-red migration would cease because blue states might become livable again, with Representative Lee Zeldin seemingly headed for a surprise victory in New York's gubernatorial race. I was writing about a blip in American history, this refugee migration, that had already run its course, and there was no point in going forward.

Of course, as the world well knows, the "Red Wave" never happened.

In the aftermath of election day, urbanologist Joel Kotkin wrote at Spiked, "Yesterday's Midterms were not a victory for conservative or progressive ideology, but an assertion of the growing power of geography in American politics. It was less a national election than a clash of civilizations."

Florida's popularity did not decline in any serious manner during the difficult economic times of late 2022 and into 2023, at least according to reports on the ground from people who are, as they say, in a position to know. One of those, Rocky Músico, a man who runs a business in the state that maintains properties for hundreds of seasonal residents, told me that real estate development is continuing apace, with no sign of a turndown in prices. To the contrary, condominium units are sprouting up everywhere, with starting buy-ins at the million-dollar level. Not long ago, he says, they were five hundred thousand. ∎

29

GORDON GEKKO IS BACK...
WITH BAD HAIR!

It was several days after the midterms that I caught up with Rocky Top over the phone.

By then another shoe had dropped—you might call it a steel-toed boot, maybe even a jackboot that stomped on the people. It became known as the FTX scandal.

FTX emerged early in our conversation when I asked Rocky Top what his big "takeaway" was from the 2022 election.

He said immediately that it was horrible, but he wasn't just opining on the depressing and unexpected electoral outcomes. The corruption of our government, he said, was far greater than anything he had ever conceived. It was a massive corruption that encompassed both political parties, only slightly less for the Republicans. He was referring not to the election itself, whatever its level of malfeasance, but to the aforementioned FTX scandal. I, already transfixed by the news reports coming out, readily agreed. This cosmic level of corruption somehow put the election, disappointing as it was, in the rearview mirror.

What took me aback was that someone with Rocky's experience in the highest levels of DC and Tennessee politics could say such a thing. I assumed he had seen it all. Apparently this was more than even he had seen—a considerable amount more, by the tone of his voice.

FTX's obvious Ponzi scheme resulted in a $32 billion loss and bankruptcy while enriching Sam Bankman-Fried, who proceeded to donate tens of millions of dollars to Democratic Party candidates (making him the party's second-largest donor after George Soros). He also gave a significantly lesser amount to the most obvious Never Trump Republicans, in order to demonstrate the phoniest of even-handedness. What Sam Bankman-Fried—the supposed "Crypto King"—and his cohort had done was outside the bounds of what could be construed as normal corruption, venturing into the realm of the surreal. This was especially odd since Bankman-Fried was a young man with a terrible haircut who dressed like a refugee from a *circa* 1967 Big Brother and the Holding Company concert. He had been holding forth with nonstop "woke" rhetoric—backing every uber-trendy cause from the Black Lives Matter/Antifa/LGBTQ2+ victimhood, the "green" everything playbook, and beyond—all while living a polymorphous perverse lifestyle in his Bahamas penthouse that would have made Janis Joplin blush.

It was the mother of all cover stories, replete with Bill Clinton sitting beside Bankman-Fried on a panel grinning like the Cheshire Cat after just having found its prey. As I wrote in the *Epoch Times*, the Mafia never dreamed of pulling off anything that daring or remunerative. The numbers were staggering.

What we were witnessing, I speculated, was the final apotheosis of the dark side of the sixties, a cultural period I had lived through and participated in, or at least identified with in some way. Bankman-Fried was the true face of progressivism. Those who had attacked the Man had now become the Man and then some. The Jacobins turned the French Revolution into a bloody internal massacre of epic proportions. These folks turned the sixties into a bizarre self-parody dominated by an avarice that would have embarrassed even Gordon "greed is good" Gekko from Oliver Stone's

Wall Street. Perhaps that was always the point. The counterculture was just a new way to make money, lots of it, with no conscience to interfere and no worries about producing a product of use to anybody. These folks didn't need Nietzsche to tell them "God is dead." As far as they were concerned, he was never alive. What an old-fashioned concept.

Where were his parents, both Stanford professors, in all this? If anything, they were more culpable than Sam. Was this the paradigm of sixties-style childrearing come home to roost? Or was it like Joe and Hunter Biden, another parent-to-child example of "hip," actually absent, childrearing? When John Lennon intoned "Imagine," his iconic anthem about a future godless nirvana, was the subliminal message of those words really, Rape and pillage all you want, because nobody's watching? This was certainly no "Spirit in the Sky." What did Janis Joplin actually mean when she sang "Get It While You Can"? The music of that era might have been great, but the lyrics implanted a very different message, yielding unprecedented selfishness and narcissism.

Those stratospheric levels of greed, flowing from the narcissism, blew Rocky Top and me away. It also meant something very obvious for the present moment. Democracy, whether small-r republican or not, cannot work in the face of scandals of this nature. The issue of votes being bought with tens of millions of dollars should dwarf concerns about Dominion machines, early ballots, ballot harvesting, and the rest of the dirty tricks that have pervaded our culture.

This kind of money was blinding, and it transformed politicians beyond recognition.

That Rocky Top recognized this meant he was, and had always been, an idealist masquerading as a snarky cynic. Maybe I was too. But what we were both looking at was nothing short of civilizational Armageddon.

Yet another outgrowth of the disappointing and inscrutable midterms was a corollary to this exceedingly depressing situation. The midterm election saw five million more Republicans vote, but the actual results were something close to a push. This data prompted the question: had the Great American Migration that inspired this book slowed, or even halted? Were there to be no more American refugees to inspire change, the way external refugees had done for previous generations? Should we give up? ∎

30

KEEP MOVING

The economy was either on the edge of recession or long beyond it, depending on which talking head you chose to listen to. Meanwhile, the once-booming real estate market was tanking as mortgage rates shot up to levels not seen in years, in near-tandem with the Federal Reserve raising rates at a breakneck pace to halt runaway inflation. By Thanksgiving 2022, it was almost impossible to tell if this was working.

I went back to real estate broker Dave Markowicz—with his offices in Franklin, Tennessee, and his erstwhile home Santa Monica, California—who had been profiting from the trend on both ends, to see how it looked to him on the ground.

I wasn't surprised that Dave had the same view I had. People's desire to move had not ceased; if anything it was greater, but their ability to move had been circumscribed by the onerous economic conditions that threatened to worsen. Who could relocate at a time when inflation was rampant and the stock market sinking? But this hadn't deterred Dave, who, like other refugees, moved forward as a political activist. He started his own website, Find Freedom, and made his debut as an author with a short, self-published book: *The New Cold War – Red and Blue – America Divided*, with the subtitle "The Escape of the Leftugee to Find Freedom."

I was hoping Dave could give me some up-to-date data, but there wasn't much to be had. This wasn't surprising when data for something as monumental as the pandemic was largely obscured—almost certainly deliberately—and several states (nearly all of them red) had been "accidentally" undercounted in the latest census, thus denying them full representation in Congress.

He did send the latest information available, a North American Van Lines report entitled "Where Are Americans Moving in 2021?," which I had previously seen. Nevertheless, it was worth reviewing. In the company's words, "The Carolinas, Tennessee, Florida, Arizona and Texas are the top destinations for movers." One wondered immediately if this was still true of Arizona, with all the unresolved electoral consternation going on in the state. It had always been a retirement haven, attractive particularly to the diminishing but still somewhat potent John McCain wing of the GOP as they reached a certain age. But that wasn't the group who normally became refugees of the type seeking constitutional republicanism. More often than not, they made peace with the woke world or became subsumed by it. A number of them were resisting the refugees and other constitutionalists in the Arizona electoral battles. In fact, they were in the leadership to preserve a reactionary, anti-citizen, elitist status quo.

But what was most interesting about the North American Van Lines report is what was conspicuously absent—the *raison d'être* for this book. The van line wishes to tell us, "The top three factors for moving in 2021 are: cost of living, proximity to family, work flexibility." Conspicuously missing was the desire, in many cases the passionate desire, to leave moribund blue states mired in a rapidly deteriorating socialistic lifestyle for red states that were freer. Indeed, such a factor was not even mentioned in the lengthy list of motivations in their survey; it's doubtful that the vassals of the cowardly corporation even dared to ask. Still, North American does some reporting by codifying the obvious with its data, reminding us that the top five states for departures are Illinois, California, New Jersey, Michigan, and New York. The company also tells us that "Over 20% more Americans are moving in 2021 compared to 2020." Did that number increase in 2022? Will it continue to grow in 2023, despite the economic forces discouraging those same departures at every turn? The costs of moving alone often well surpass any tax savings, immediate ones in any case. Again, we don't know.

What we do know is that the "woke" corporations, tech or otherwise, and our "woke" government don't want to tell us anything substantive. Their doctrines of ESG (environmental, social, and governance) and SDG (sustainable development goals) militate against the people having any real knowledge of what is happening. Consciously or not, the socialist/communist/statist ideal is what the refugees were fleeing. There would be no "Great Reset" for them, but as the country deteriorated socially and economically, they would have to adjust.

How would this widening conflict resolve itself? Was a new, more extreme, detailed, and negotiated form of federalism the answer? If so, could it be achieved?

Rocky Top and I discussed this once more over lunch at an Asian fusion restaurant in an upscale Nashville suburb. The place was filled with seemingly affluent patrons, despite the downturn. Were they fiddling while Rome burned? It made me think of *Dr. Zhivago*, particularly those scenes where a once-magnificent home had been carved up, the furniture broken apart for firewood. Nothing was the same. Would Zhivago ever meet Lara again in a brutally impoverished socialist world? Nevertheless, at this particular restaurant, the band played on (figuratively) while patrons chowed down on house-made organic fried rice, their choice of protein, and extra miso sauce on the side.

Outside, everything had become more complicated on a daily basis. Had we reached the intractable moment? Rocky and I wondered.

Was a second civil war now looming? The academic pundit F. H. Buckley was recently quoted as saying if such a war broke out, the North, with all its weapons, would win once again.

Rocky, less the academic and more the boots-on-the-ground, hard-nosed politico, thought differently. The South had more than its share of military installations. I concurred, noting that the military rank-and-file might well sympathize with the South over the military's tiresome "woke" leadership.

Nevertheless, we both still agreed we didn't want a civil war to happen. But what next?

That night, on *Tucker Carlson Tonight*, Elon Musk's revelations about Twitter started to roll in, demonstrating just how far the Democratic Party operatives and the Biden administration had gone in forming a network between Tech and the government. These documents were what in the *Epoch Times* I named the "Twitter Papers" (in homage to the Pentagon Papers), but which were eventually referred to as the "Twitter Files." Big Tech and the FBI colluded to repress all potent conservative thought or news of their extreme corruption, such as the Hunter Biden laptop affair, from reaching the populace of our country, freedom of speech be damned.

What next, indeed?

One answer to the question was that the people—despite difficult economic times, lockdowns, and so forth—were still on the move, voting with their feet, as the saying goes, but actually with their U-Haul, Penske, and Ryder rental trucks.

Just a month or so after my latest colloquy with Rocky Top, the new statistics came out from the US Census. For the third year in a row the population of California had declined, something that had never happened to the ever-expanding Golden State before 2020. From April 1, 2020, to July 1, 2022, California had gone from 39,538,245 persons to 39,029,342. New York has had an even steeper population decline.

Meanwhile, Texas, Florida, North Carolina, Georgia, Arizona, South Carolina, and Tennessee all gained a significant number of citizens.

And these statistics come from the government, making it possible, or even likely, that they are skewed in favor of the blue states, as the Heritage Foundation's Hans von Spakovsky has demonstrated they have been in previous years.

In 1966's "For What It's Worth" Buffalo Springfield told us what was "happening." Many think of this as an era entirely different from our own. In reality, it may have been the true beginning of what we are experiencing now—the formation of two countries within one, with different values and different goals, almost two entirely different ways of life.

Meanwhile, a photo that looked like an outtake from the *Beverly Hillbillies* was making the rounds of people's text messages and chat rooms. The legend printed over it was "They said 'Calforny is the place we gotta flee' / So they packed up the truck and moved back to Tennessee." ∎

31

"PAULA REVERE" RIDES AGAIN IN THE GULCH

S ince it's a boom town—or, as it's been called, the "It City"—
Nashville has several trendy neighborhoods. East Nashville is
our Brooklyn. Sylvan Park is our version of LA's Silver Lake; the
Nations neighborhood is up-and-coming in a manner that reminds
one of Echo Park. (You could add an emphatic "sort of" to all of
these comparisons, because none of these Nashville neighborhoods
is anywhere near as large as the originals.)

The foregoing is home to both families and singles, but for
singles, the most desired location seems to be the neighborhood
known as the Gulch, with its chic hotels, high-end fashion boutiques, and the latest restaurants. Unfortunately, it's filled with
ambitious millennials who, in this day and age, are among the
most conformist generations in the history of our country, with
their adherence to the Democratic Party and their unquestion-
ing belief in anything they read in the *New York Times* or hear on
network television. (Most do not bother with the *Tennessean*, for
good reason.) These are the clones of the same people you might
meet in similar neighborhoods of most of our major cities, but
they have come to Nashville because it is a land of opportunity
and, for the moment, hip.

This did not deter (or maybe it attracted) Jaclyn Colbeth, whom I mentioned before, a single woman in her early forties who enjoys the same restaurants, bars, and boutiques. Formerly an employee of media giant Condé Nast, she rejected being around many of these same people in New York and San Diego but chose to be with their spiritual cousins in the Gulch, where, she tells me, she is very happy.

Why? She's another activist of a sort, and I have concluded, after talking to a number now, that being an activist makes you happy. In fact, it may be one of the best routes to personal fulfillment because, frustrating as it nearly always is, you feel you are contributing to a better world, in Colbeth's case among the young, rich, and ambitious.

Colbeth sees herself as "Paula Revere," come to warn these denizens of the Gulch: "The Marxists are coming!" She does this in small meetings, where she tells them what the future of cities will be like if they don't pay attention—no one with cars, everyone living in small cubicles, families dispersed and irrelevant, children (if any) raised by a "village" (to paraphrase Hillary Clinton) and not by their parents. You'll own nothing and, instead of the happiness promised by Klaus Schwab, you'll experience misery and anomie while your overlords remain rich as Croesus. Welcome to the Great Reset.

Colbeth is a brave woman, going directly into the belly of the beast. She is dealing with what we might call the Lifestyles of the Young and Brainwashed. And she is only a recent refugee, having come to Tennessee in early 2022. More power to her.

Generally speaking, these refugees could be classified in basic waves. Colbeth is what I would call a fourth-wave refugee. The first wave began somewhat indeterminately, but before the second wave, *circa* 2018, when Sheryl and I arrived. Then came the third wave—during COVID. This one was heavier. Jaclyn Colbeth is part of that post-COVID wave, which occurred when the pandemic was on the wane, at least domestically. Will there be a fifth? Maybe it's already taking place. ∎

32

MY WIFE, THE SCREENWRITER, TURNS POLITICAL ORGANIZER

When you travel cross-country for a new life, you may be surprised, even astonished, by what becomes of you, what your reaction will be to the collision of your personality and character with a strikingly different culture.

This was especially true, it seemed to me, if you came "unarmed," i.e., without any particular work assignment to divert and anchor you. You were, in essence, winging it.

I was armed in the sense that I had a job writing for PJ Media and shortly thereafter for the *Epoch Times*. This was something I could do from almost anywhere, given the far-reaching digital arms of the internet. They weren't particularly warm arms, but they were always there, as long as the power grid held out.

Sheryl Longin, my wife, had a strong writing life of her own, having coauthored the screenplay for the well-received *Dick*, a quirky comedy in which two teenage girls (Nixon's dog walkers no less) turned out to be "Deep Throat" in the Watergate scandal. She had collaborated with me as well on the independent feature *Prague Duet*. Sheryl had further written a fair amount of journalism for outlets like *Interview* and *Vanity Fair*.

Nevertheless, by the time we were moving cross-country, much of that part of her life had been in abeyance for a while in favor of concentrating on raising our daughter, Madeleine. Yet Madeleine herself was growing up, already gone through college at honor student level and then on to a one-year rapid MBA at Nashville's Belmont University—all this in the midst of the COVID lockdown insanity. She was now working full-time in a responsible job for an important international finance company. Mother had reared her daughter well.

But this left Sheryl, as I said, temporarily unarmed, at least in the work area. The novelty of living in a totally new environment diverted us both for a while, but that could only go on for so long.

Then, serendipitously really, Jane Whitson, a blogger and journalist, invited Sheryl to join her at the monthly luncheon of the Nashville Republican Women. I knew Whitson, who lived in Nashville, via PJ Media long before we moved, and via her blog, the wittily named Webutante.

Nashville Republican Women, as it happened, was the oldest and in many ways the most powerful of GOP organizations in the area, though largely composed of women of a "certain age" and split between old-line conventional Republicans and MAGA-leaning conservatives.

Sheryl started attending the luncheons, and I even spoke at one or two. Sheryl rapidly became, by the force of her personality and her intelligence, a leader in the organization. Soon she was the vice president (she might even have been president, if she had wanted the role) and was in charge of booking the monthly speakers for the group.

Without realizing it, in our small ways we were doing our best to follow Benjamin Franklin's instruction, "Either write something worth reading or do something worth writing."

Sheryl was doing just that, because the essential activity of the Nashville Republican Women was their monthly speaker program.

The old guard wanted the conventional GOP politicians, most of whom had a RINO tint stemming from years of bipartisan—some call it "uniparty"—collegiality. Or was it collaboration? Either way, it was a dubious Tennessee tradition, masking what was largely a business coalition to keep money in the same hands it had been in for generations, or alternatively in the hands of a new donor class naturally attracted to one of the most rapidly growing metropolitan areas in the country.

So, at the leadership level, the Nashville Left wouldn't take things too far if their mirror on the right agreed to behave similarly. Trump had won this state by two-thirds. Tennessee was a MAGA state, but much of its Republican leadership was anything but. Sheryl, in her way, was endeavoring to fix that, or at least make an impact.

Speaking up for the "woke" Left, however, was the bloated forty-one-member Nashville Metro Council, whose meetings were available for view on local television. Watching them on the small screen, one felt that the antics of this council rivalled those of Monty Python in sheer absurdity. Ultimately, the Metro Council was a ragtag collection of idealistic, would-be Trotskyites that, in practice, functioned as a daffy rubber stamp for the mayor, who kept these crazy lefties on a short leash, in order that they would support those same business interests. Lately that meant building a huge new football stadium for the Tennessee Titans, retractable roof and all, to attract the Super Bowl. The projected cost is $2.2 billion, mostly paid with public funds, though no taxpayer had a chance to vote for it. The chances it will stay within budget are next to none.

This all took place under the guise of "business as usual." Sheryl took a different approach, inviting more challenging speakers to the Nashville Republican Women luncheons. These included gadfly state senator Janice Bowling; Lee Smith, the famed author and journalist who helped unmask the Russia hoax, and who is also an expert in critical race theory and other left-wing excrescences infecting the school system; and the newly appointed Tennessee attorney general Jonathan Skrmetti, a leader in fighting the good fight for states' rights and a constitutionally sound federalism, thus weakening the diktats of the Biden administration.

These free-thinking speakers were not always applauded by the old guard in the organization. Where were the familiar politicians and their comfortable, self-serving speeches that made those ladies feel equally comfortable and "inside" as they pecked daintily at their catered salads at the Hillwood Country Club? Nevertheless, Sheryl and others soldiered on, bringing new blood and, more importantly, fresh ideas into the club.

They and the Young Republican Club members—many of whom we knew from the Fifth Congressional debate—were attempting to revive the moribund Davidson County Republican Party, and are continuing to do so. While not entirely a refugee-versus-old-guard battle, there is a strong element of that dynamic. Some of the old guard joined the insurgents, including longtime Nashville resident but newly elected SEC member Lulu Elam. A coalition of different activist groups are returning the Republican Party to its voters—to the people. For some time, local party organizations have acted as ineffective social clubs, headed by what seem like deliberately incompetent leaders. The real power resides with the politicians and their array of strategists who, in many ways, have more power than the politicians themselves. It's time to change that. Tennessee is an interesting testing ground to see if this can be accomplished. It will take great, determined people to do it. I have met several such people, but the one who impressed me most, a paradigm of the ideal conservative/constitutionalist activist, was Kathleen Harms. ∎

33

PORTRAIT OF AN ACTIVIST
AS A MIDDLE-AGED WOMAN

The first time I walked into the Cordell Hull Building in downtown Nashville, where most of the elected officials in the Tennessee Assembly have their offices, with the middle-aged, attractive blonde Kathy Harms, I knew I was with the real deal.

I could tell by the way those officials looked at her, some with welcoming pleasure, others with only lightly disguised dread. The latter were almost invariably those closest to the upper echelons of government.

Though the woman is unfailingly polite, she is indefatigable. She leaves no stone unturned in her search for justice, particularly in the area of election integrity. On this topic, Harms argues that "We have been gaslit by everybody, whether it's the secretary of state, the state coordinator of elections, some of our legislators and even, unintentionally, Heritage Action for America." She could add almost every authority in almost every state.

Harms has been promoting for some time a petition that reads: "I, the undersigned, do not consent to the use of electronic voting systems to cast and tabulate my vote." It further stipulates the use of "only currency grade, control numbered hand marked paper ballots to authenticate the ballot."

Why not? It works for the French in their elections, and it would resolve a lot of questions about ours. The French figure out their election results more quickly than we do.

Harms barnstormed Tennessee on this issue in the company of Gary Humble of Tennessee Stands, Garland Favorito of VoterGA, and Representative Andy Ogles before he was elected to Congress.

But it's not just election integrity. On virtually every concern relevant to grassroots conservatives, from education to the border, Harms is in the forefront, knocking on the doors of powerful and ordinary citizens alike.

If you knew Kathy Harms and her husband, Tom, as I do, you would wonder where this gentle woman found her moxie. No wonder her emails have, at bottom, a quotation borrowed, spiritually though not ideologically, from the Gray Panthers' Maggie Kuhn: "Speak the Truth Even If Your Voice Shakes."

I have never heard Harms's voice shake, but I wondered how such a brave person evolved, so I asked her to send me a bit of her history.

The Harmses were both raised in the Midwest and went to college in Michigan. They eventually moved to Massachusetts, where Tom worked successfully in the corporate world and Kathy homeschooled their two children. At the same time, she served on the boards of various nonprofits, and she worked with her husband as a team on one. To enhance this work, she enrolled in Gordon Cornwell Theological Seminary for her master's. This is where she discovered the Marxist roots of liberation theology and saw the social justice movement looming ominously on the horizon. It was a turning point.

When Tom retired in 2007, the Harmses decided it was time to leave New England, although, in her words, it had "captured their hearts." A visit to Tennessee "felt like home... At that time, TN was more affordable, family friendly, and appeared to be a true 'red state.'" She continued in email that she hoped "that the southern sensibilities of faith and family would be a port in the storm from the burgeoning Marxist philosophy infecting faith and family 'up north.'" Instead, however, they have found that "Tennessee, despite its charms, was as susceptible to the same deceptions." She was not sure if this was a result of Tennessee's "naivete" or "the political prowess of the ruling elite that is pulling a hard left." The Harmses, she wrote, "have driven down roots and intend to defend [their] vision of faith, family, and freedom in the middle of America: Tennessee."

I'm not sure I would quite use the term "hard left," but perhaps that's my own naivete. ∎

34

PLAYING TENNIS WITH A GUY CALLED BUBBA

Although I wish it were otherwise, I'm only a mediocre club tennis player. Yet in a certain sense I owe my life to the sport. I have been active as both fan and participant since roughly the age of seven. It was then I discovered I was too short to play my beloved basketball with any success. My attempted layups were being stuffed down my throat.

I also noted in those days—it's no longer remotely true—that some of the greatest tennis players in the world, like the amazing Australian duo Rod Laver and Ken Rosewall, were also "altitude challenged." I tried the game and found that I wasn't bad because I had decent hand-eye coordination.

Tennis became my game and, since it's a lifetime sport, I am extremely grateful for that. I recently encountered online studies from Denmark and Britain demonstrating that tennis was by far the best activity—better than jogging, weight lifting, even swimming—to promote longevity. The Danish study found that tennis extended your life close to an extraordinary ten years. I hope it's correct.

In the process of moving to Nashville, one of the first things I asked our realtor, as she drove us around town looking at properties, was where and with whom I could play tennis. As it happened, the woman, a knowledgeable and generous fount of local information, had an immediate answer. Her friend Don Greene, who was my age and with whom she and her husband had dinner regularly, played tennis five times a week. She would introduce me.

Five times a week? That was a serious amount of tennis if you weren't a pro. He must be retired, I thought. He wasn't. He just found time to get in a lot of tennis. It turned out he was a terrific guy and helped me get into the country club where he played, literally within weeks of my moving.

Shortly thereafter, I was playing several times a week with a group of men who were also mostly close to my age, with a few younger players to remind us, as if we needed it, that we weren't twenty-five anymore. They were mostly businessmen and mostly evangelical Christians, but they welcomed me, a Jew from California, without hesitation. New blood was always needed to make sure there would be enough players for a couple of hours of doubles.

As happened with Todd Homme, the California refugee I mentioned earlier who found his way into local society through hockey, it was already becoming clear to me that love of a sport was a gift, especially to men, like me, who were in the midst of a transition. Once on the court, I was no longer a refugee from some Yankee state. Instead, I was just another guy trying to find the seams of the ball.

It only got better, because playing a sport with the same people over time, over four years now in this case, gives rise to a considerable degree of camaraderie and mutual trust. One man (Robert) was our car guy, another real estate (John), yet another was the organizer (Ron), and so forth. One of the semi-regulars was called Bubba. This was a down-home name I never in my old life would have associated with tennis—seems more fit for football—but he turned out to be an excellent player.

After a while, these men, as noted evangelicals and almost uniformly conservatives, would ask me in confidence why so many Jews didn't like Israel. (Several of them had been there, some multiple times, and loved the country.) I would usually make a joke in response, an indication of how deeply the question struck home. Sometimes, however, I would do my best to explain the division in my religion. A lot of Jewish leftism, I'd explain, stemmed from the days of the Bolsheviks and a hope for an atheistic world where, theoretically, no one could be discriminated against for their beliefs. Of course, it didn't turn out that way—a lot of things don't. Trying to be optimistic, I would point out that the secular Jews were beginning to die out through assimilation. The secular also had low birth rates, very low in fact, compared to the religious, who followed God's admonition to be fruitful and multiply. They would be the dominant force in the Jewish religion in the not-too-distant future. In Israel that seems to have already happened.

Not surprisingly, the only liberal in our group of players was also the only other Jew. At the beginning, we would quarrel with each other frequently, sometimes vociferously and to the detriment of the game. That died down when we ended up playing on the same side in some team competitions against other clubs, necessitating our taking our tennis more seriously than our ideologies. I learned something from that about keeping politics out of where it doesn't belong. Politics ruined sports. It had happened on the national scale, with broadcasters on ESPN and various famous athletes unable to keep from airing their political beliefs to the world. These dimwitted lectures, often delivered under the mantle of social justice, sometimes extended to approving the actions of despots.

But knowing this same man was instructive in a different way. Our mutual religion aside, he was a living example of just how separated the two Americas had become. One day, in the midst of a game when political chatter once again leaked out—it must have been some hot news event—the other players and I discovered he had not heard of John Durham, the attorney charged with leading the investigation of the Russia hoax. All of us were flabbergasted. How was that possible? Here was an intelligent fellow, a graduate of an Ivy League college with an engineering degree, who had started his own company. The investigation had already been going on for years, with nearly nightly reports on Fox. It must have been reported somewhere in the *New York Times*—or was it always buried on page 25? Such were the silos that we lived in. The man has since left Tennessee and moved north, and political chatter has receded among the tennis players, except for nervous talk concerning the direction of our country, about which we are all in agreement.

This makes tennis, though just a game, all the more important, and the unspoken camaraderie all the greater. I know if I were ever in a pinch, these men would have my back (as I would have theirs), even if, compared to most of them who were born, raised, and educated in Tennessee, I was a relative interloper, a refugee. They would also, I suspect, despite their age, have firearms waiting in their lockers and closets to save our republic, were it to come to that. ∎

35

THE ARRIVAL OF A NEW FORM
OF MEN'S GROUP

Back in the sixties and seventies, a phenomenon known as "Men's Consciousness Raising Groups" was emerging in the big cities. This was in response to the "Women's Consciousness Raising Groups" proliferating everywhere as an outgrowth of the women's liberation movement of that time.

I was then a member of what was said to be the first Men's Consciousness Raising Group in Los Angeles. I don't know if it really raised consciousnesses, but it was an interesting assembly of mostly ambitious young men, one of whom went on to run Universal Studios for a time. Another became a successful producer of a series of action movies involving endless car crashes. The conversation was not, however, very liberationist or even liberal (or, for that matter, very political at all), though everyone there was leftist or nearly so, and despite the group's origin as the companion to a highly activist women's group.

In reality the group became a relatively secret enclave of business connections and sexual discussion, during which deals were made and romantic assignations bragged about. One of the men, who claimed to be in an "open marriage," was even having a flagrant affair with the significant other of another man in the group.

Whether this very public affair (which was of course humiliating to the individual being cuckolded) was what we would today call "politically correct" became the primary topic of discussion for our weekly meetings in excruciating detail. The group was, in a sense, a harbinger of the left-wing/woke hypocrisy we see all around us now. In all candor, I too was, to some degree, a willing participant in this immoral madness. That was the temper of the times. It wasn't long, however, before I could no longer stand it and stopped going. I wasn't the only one who dropped out; the group dissolved shortly thereafter.

So, decades later, when I had the opportunity to join men's groups that had sprung up near me in Tennessee's Davidson and Williamson Counties, I was leery, even though they were of a totally different sort. It must have been some kind of bad association with "men's groups" as an idea keeping me away. Or maybe it was that I was still basically a Groucho Marxist, never wanting to join a club that would have me as a member. But I had become aware of the existence of these groups—many of them formed of and by migrants from California and other blue states—and I knew that, if only to help research this book, I would have to make more than a perfunctory appearance.

Some met early in the morning in Westhaven, and so were what we used to call in Los Angeles "geographically undesirable." I just couldn't make it in time on a regular basis. But I did manage a couple of visits and found the members, largely consisting of men of a certain age, several retired military veterans, to be dedicated conservatives, eager to join together to find means of confronting the increasingly leftist culture.

I did start to attend, on a relatively regular basis, a group that had recently formed and met at the Standard, a downtown Nashville restaurant and club housed in the 1881 Smith House, a Victorian edifice that is among the oldest buildings still operating in the city. On offer to accompany the group's meetings were the establishment's manly larder of bourbon, cigars, and steak. What was not to like about that? (Well, the cigar smoke did prove to be a hazard to some, including me, after an hour or two.)

The assemblage was unofficially called the Gentlemen's Group and officially the Gentlemen of Letters and Swords, so some of the members showed up appropriately in jacket and tie, as almost always did its founder, Chuck Pierce. Pierce, a businessman, tall and well dressed, was a recent transplant to the Nashville region, starting this particular branch just after he arrived in the area in March 2021. He had launched the first branch of the Gentlemen's Group at Beverly Hills' Grand Havana Room back in 2014, and it was still going strong. I had known that place well for some time, since I went there often with my very liberal Hollywood agent, who kept a stash of expensive cigars in the private club—as many industry fat cats did and presumably still do—in his own personal locked humidor. If I had only known that Pierce, the furthest thing from a liberal, would later convene there, I might well have joined his group before I left California four years later in 2018.

With various fits and starts, Pierce, who seems to have national intentions and already has a YouTube channel, initiated other gentlemen's groups in Dallas and Orange County, California. He failed in Alexandria, Virginia, because the local cigar club, in his words, "didn't like us talking history and politics"—inside the Beltway, no less.

These gentlemen's club meetings, though friendly and cordial, are, at base, quite serious, and its discussions are intellectually rigorous. Pierce is a particularly strong historian.

I asked him to explain his goals for the group:

> I thought men need camaraderie, intellectual stimulation, friend-ship and fellowship...together just men in a room talking about ideals, political philosophy, culture, and history. Men make other men stronger.

I did not think men were reading enough or gathering together enough. I also thought America was becoming feminized and the way to at least have an impact was to get men in a room together, smoking cigars talking about ideals, philosophy, culture, and history.

I think men need to know history.

Amen to that. I imagine we could say everybody needs to know history. Nevertheless, this was a far cry from my old seventies hippy-dippy men's consciousness raising group. This was true consciousness raising. Here members gained a greater understanding of the past, so that they would not, in George Santayana's well-known words, be "condemned to repeat it."

Held once a month (although many of the members seemed to be constantly in touch via online group chats), the gatherings began with that camaraderie over whiskey and cigars until Pierce would call us to order. He would then read, sometimes at great length—thankfully he is a decent orator—something historical: a document, a letter, a portion of a book, whatever. Usually, it was easy to see its contemporary relevance, but not so much its provenance—who wrote it and when.

Pierce would go around the room and ask us to guess what it was. A few times some of the members were able to. One member, John Wilson, a sound engineer we had drafted for the congressional debate, wasn't bad at that. I was terrible. I even missed George Washington's Farewell Address to the United States Senate, an extraordinarily sophisticated speech the likes of which we haven't heard in decades, possibly longer. I also whiffed on an excerpt from the works of Friedrich Hayek when, for years, I went around saying the Austrian-British economist's *The Road to Serfdom* had, more than any other book, changed my political views from left to right. It was a bit embarrassing, especially since I was usually the only published author there. My shame would disappear quickly, however, in the ensuing welter of discussion that could go on far into the night.

Largely because of Pierce's presence in Tennessee—a state he says "values the free markets and principles that made America the city on a hill," as opposed to his former residence in California "that was in decline as I saw it and headed more and more away from those principles"—Nashville and environs have become the center of a movement that aims to expand to as many groups as it can across the country. Already Music City has welcomed two "gentlemen's conferences," the first in October 2021 and the second in October 2022, which I attended, with members coming from the other groups across the country.

Some of the same men, Pierce tells me, have been coming to these groups for years. He sent me statements from these members, such as Jack S., which speak to the value of this time spent socializing: "Men become better men when they spend time together. They become better citizens, friends, fathers, and leaders. In a world where manliness and masculinity are scoffed at as relics of a bygone era, groups like [this] create supportive environment[s] where men can bond and learn from other men, becoming better men in the process."

Or this one from another man, who also happens to be named Jack: "Chuck Pierce is a dynamic, inspiring leader who had the vision to start this brotherhood of American Gentlemen that has created a culture to change this declining one with this positive and dynamic movement. We get together to smoke cigars, eat, and drink just as the Founding Fathers did in Taverns of old that created this great American Republic. Chuck has the vision and the business plan to make huge change in our culture."

When I first attended these meetings, I was, as I said, skeptical. Though I am more or less an intellectual sort, it seemed unlikely that these historical discussions might cause significant change in a society increasingly dominated by the mind-control of Big Tech,

Big Pharma, and the rest of the Great Reset crew.

Yet there was no question that the problem of men in our culture is real and drastic, as I came to understand years ago from the work of my friend, Knoxville resident Dr. Helen Smith, author of *Men on Strike: Why Men Are Boycotting Marriage, Fatherhood and the American Dream—and Why It Matters.*

Men are checking out everywhere, not going to college—maybe they shouldn't; maybe nobody should—holing up in their parents' basement playing computer games or becoming so depressed that only suicide or fentanyl, two sides of the same coin, seem attractive to them. White men in particular are regularly, almost ritually, accused of "white supremacy" or "sexual abuse" before they have even said a word or stepped out their front door. The once-respected paterfamilias is a joke on virtually every television show and commercial.

Chuck Pierce is clearly onto something. With men crashing, society inevitably crashes with them. His men are, of course, nowhere near as badly off as those poor wretches in the basement, but you have to start somewhere, with the willing and interested, to bring our sex back to something resembling self-respect. Pierce, a refugee himself, is already to be applauded for his brave, though still limited, attempt. We can only root for him to keep going and move on to greater success. His YouTube channel is titled "Restoring Men and History with Chuck Pierce." Not that surprisingly, on his website, we find the words of the man many believe most inspired the Founding Fathers, John Locke: "Education begins the gentleman, but reading, good company and reflection must finish him." ∎

36

BORIS, THE DOUBLE REFUGEE

I first met Boris Zelkin and his wife, Deeji, sometime in early 1996, I think. My wife, Sheryl, and I were putting together our independent, Holocaust-themed feature *Prague Duet*, and we were looking for a composer. Boris, who often collaborated with Deeji on their compositions, was recommended by mutual friends. They said he was a fabulous musician who could work in many genres from classical to pop. He was young at the time, without much in the way of credits, and I was nervous, as I was something of a neophyte director myself. Maybe the fact that he was born in Moscow, Russia (not to be confused with Moscow, Idaho), and was, in the company of his parents, a refugee from Soviet oppression at a very young age prompted me to take a risk and hire him.

It turned out to have been a good decision. *Prague Duet* had something of a checkered career, as do the majority of independent films. Without going into details that are not germane to this book, I deserve my part of the blame for its limited successes. But Boris's, and to some degree Deeji's, work on the film was exceptional. It was a thrilling moment when, roughly two years later, we returned to the Czech Republic to record his score with the Prague Symphony Orchestra.

After that, Boris and I remained friends even as our careers diverged. He scored a few more movies, but for the most part he was composing the background music for sporting events like the World Figure Skating Championship. It wasn't his original intention—he wasn't particularly a sports fan—but it was honest work and a decent living.

When I would visit him, I sensed a certain discontent. Because this was Hollywood, I at first assumed it was the usual career frustration exacerbated by envy that nearly everybody experienced, almost to the point of monomania—why wasn't I chosen to do whatever for Spielberg's latest movie?—but I was wrong. What was really bothering Boris was the education of his son, and therefore the boy's future.

Boris, you see, had another, non-musical, more academic or literary side, and he was writing occasional pieces for conservative websites like American Greatness and Real Clear Politics. Although he was modest to a fault about this, he was a more than passably decent writer, expressing his libertarian views in a voice that could be described as gentlemanly. Nevertheless, these efforts were already becoming risky in the entertainment industry, where an unwritten blacklist of anyone even slightly right of center was beginning to prevail, especially those who were foolish enough to publicize their views.

Boris and Deeji's son had been attending the Mirman School in West Los Angeles, founded in 1962 as a kindergarten through eighth grade institution for highly gifted children. Since their son was intellectually precocious and a rapid learner—not surprising considering his parents—it had seemed the right choice at the time. Unfortunately, as those times changed, and although the rhetoric on the school's website remained relatively banal and inoffensive, the actual behavior of the institution was altering significantly, veering to the woke left along with the Hollywood community and much of greater Los Angeles. It wasn't yet at the level of "acknowledge your 'white supremacy' twenty-four seven and repent" (a demand that perplexed Boris, whose family had had to endure generations of antisemitism in Russia), but it was getting close.

Boris and Deeji were alarmed at what they were hearing from their son and soon found themselves at loggerheads with the school's faculty and administration, urging them to return to their original purpose—even-handed education, not propaganda. But again, given the temper of the times, this was going nowhere. As Sheryl and I had, and at just about the same time, Boris and Deeji were discovering they no longer, in the words of Randy Newman's once-inspirational song played endlessly at Lakers games, "loved LA." It was time to leave.

First and foremost, Boris and Deeji looked around online for a place with a school they felt would better fit their son. In that search they discovered the Great Hearts Academies, classical education public charter schools (ergo, free to all) that were proliferating across many states. One of those was in Phoenix, where it happened to be "the highest-performing network of schools, both charter and district, in the entire Phoenix-metro area," according to its website. As it also happened, Deeji's aging parents were looking for a place to live. Bingo.

Boris Zelkin became a refugee twice—first, as a child, from the former Soviet Union to the USA; second, as an adult, from California to Arizona.

I contacted him recently for this book, realizing that I had not covered his new state sufficiently. I had attended meetings here in Tennessee, arranged by Kathleen Harms and others, with activist Arizona officials like Mark Finchem. Still, I remained baffled by the seemingly nonstop electoral corruption in its Maricopa County, by far the state's most populous county (which included Metro Phoenix), not to mention the consternation surrounding the failed gubernatorial campaign of Kari Lake.

I was hoping Boris could help me understand this better, but, surprisingly, in our Zoom call he didn't appear to have more than a routine interest. He had moved on from the quotidian hurly-burly of politics, local or otherwise, to more eternal questions. I was contacting an older and wiser Boris.

This evolution happened through his son. Boris was so beguiled by the education the boy was receiving at the Great Hearts charter school that he decided he wanted to teach there himself. After the requisite training, he was doing just that. He was teaching "Humane Letters" to eleventh and twelfth graders. The eleventh-grade syllabus ran from the Greeks (Sophocles, Homer) to the Hebrew Bible, with a required Shakespeare play at the end of the year, in this case *Hamlet.* For the twelfth graders it began with Rome and ran through Dostoevsky, with stops for the likes of Augustine, Aquinas, and Machiavelli in between. The conclusion for seniors was *King Lear.*

To call this magnificent brain food for young people, especially compared to the woke pabulum currently being served in most public schools, is a titanic understatement. It also had, as the classics almost always do, tremendous modern ramifications. Boris recounted how this worked, describing how a class on Thucydides engendered a two-hour conversation among the students about to what degree the personal lives of our leaders should affect our judgment of them.

I asked him who the students' parents were, thinking they would mostly be conservative. Boris said he did not know and, on the occasions he had met them, never asked. That was not his concern. He was presenting and encouraging—requiring, it turned out—students to read and discuss acknowledged classics. It was up to the individual ultimately to decide what he or she should think. Boris seemed excited by what he was doing and appeared totally engaged. (I was learning from my former employee here—not for the first time.)

I finally asked Boris whether he missed Hollywood. Not for one day, he said. ■

37

MEETING MARSHA

I admit that I was not a very typical American refugee, if there was such a thing. I was not an anonymous or relatively private person who, fed up with life in his blue home state, migrated to a red one. While far from a "celebrity" in the *New York Post* Page Six sense of the word, I was in some way a public person for many years in different guises, from mystery novelist to screenwriter to founder of a media company some regard as pioneering—PJ Media—and now to opinion columnist at the *Epoch Times.*

Nevertheless, the degree to which I was welcomed in Tennessee was a bit surprising. Not long after our arrival, through friends, Sheryl and I were having dinner with Senator Marsha Blackburn and her stylish, bow-tied husband, Chuck Blackburn. We soon became friends of theirs as well.

Now Marsha, as was clear then but is even clearer now, is a far more public figure than even many other senators, let alone me. This is because she appears, more frequently than most politicians, on television—presumably due, in part, to her good looks and her readiness to do it. Her fame on the right and notoriety on the left grew yet greater when, during the Judiciary Committee hearings on the nomination of Ketanji Brown Jackson for associate justice of the Supreme Court, she asked the nominee to define the word "woman" and got a word salad of pseudo-scientific gobbledygook from Jackson. This exchange was featured repeatedly on conservative media, as well it should have been, and provided some of the impetus for Matt Walsh's successful documentary on the transgenderism fixation.

In late 2022, she scored another notable victory, helping lead the way in the fight to end the vaccine mandates in our military.

But none of this, I was to discover, protected her from what seemed to be a certain amount of carping from right-wing activists. Many of these were migrants from California and elsewhere, but more than a few were old-timers, even old friends of hers. She was all talk and little action, they said. Some of the time I was even disposed to agree to an extent, but our friendship far outweighed it. You could call me a compromised journalist for that, but then I would argue that virtually all in the Fourth Estate are compromised to one degree or another. It comes with the impetus to impose your views on others. Even-handedness is a facade.

This same carping about Blackburn, however, belied her pre-senatorial past when, as a state official, she was instrumental in one of the biggest political wins ever in Tennessee: preventing the imposition of a state income tax. This ended up being great for Tennessee, making it more attractive to business, allowing it to remain among the most financially stable states in the country, eventually attracting those same refugees, my family among them. Blackburn was also, as I almost immediately learned after meeting her, behind legislation to allow songwriters—who proliferate almost as much in Metro Nashville as screenwriters do, or did, in Los Angeles—to keep more of the earnings from their creations.

But among the most interesting parts of knowing Tennessee's senior senator was the insight it gave me, limited though it was, into exactly what it meant to be a senator of the minority party. To be blunt, I began to realize that it wasn't as great a job as I had assumed. The familiar catchline "world's greatest deliberative body" that had long been attached to the US Senate seemed largely mythological when, in 90 percent (or more) of cases, a senator in the minority can do almost no productive legislative work. One is left, instead, to blockade the legislation of the majority party, or simply to keep the home fires burning via public statements in the media. That's a long way from the "world's greatest deliberative body"—not that other nations' systems are any better. The Brits' "question time" for their prime minister can be highly entertaining, but the ensuing "deliberations" are often even less fruitful than ours.

The refugees, those with whom I sometimes identify anyway, were unsatisfied. As they crossed the country for new and greener grass, and then, to varying degrees, were disappointed by what they found, entrenched politicians like Blackburn, fairly or unfairly, drew much of the brunt of their discontent.

Those politicians were caught up in a familiar situation. The old saw that "money is the mother's milk of politics" turned out to be a monumental understatement. Money had become something more akin to the crack, meth, and fentanyl of politics. Big Tech and Big Pharma had access to virtually unlimited funds, and they used these to exert a dominance over legislation to a degree that no one could have imagined. To continue the above analogy, these high-tech multinational companies were the pusher men—the drug dealers feeding our politicians' addictions to the almighty dollar. These crippling relationships prevented almost all politicians—including, at times, Tennessee's two well-meaning senators, Blackburn and Hagerty—from following through on a longstanding popular demand from their constituents: serious restraints on the tech and pharma giants.

One such popular request was the restraint of the notorious Section 230, which allowed Google, Facebook, and the rest of the multinational digital oligarchs to host any link or content they wanted, as if they had nothing to do with that information's standing within their platform. In fact, the reverse was true—they had everything to do with it. They were able to choose, through their algorithms, what they thought was the important content to highlight for virtually any purpose—without fear of litigation. This made them by far the most powerful journalistic outlets in the world, yet they didn't have to acknowledge this or take responsibility for those powers. Big Tech's unfettered freedom to shape the public conversation allowed it to exert mind control at levels heretofore never imagined.

Blackburn has been a public critic of Section 230, but unable, due to her minority position, to do much about it. Some, notably Florida's DeSantis, dared to take on Big Pharma and Big Tech with real legislation. These figures, however, were the exception that proved the rule, although an alliance of red-state attorneys general, including Tennessee's recently appointed Skrmetti, provided some cause for hope.

For the refugees, this political bait and switch—having been lured to a red-state promised land only to be confronted by local politicians whose interests often bent more toward self-preservation and personal gain—fomented the development of numerous independent conservative/libertarian political organizations. The refugees also found the traditional party system, on the state and county levels, to be somewhere between useless and incompetent, consumed by minor-league matters of self-interest.

No political group could have been more incompetent than the Davidson County Republican Party. Davidson is contiguous with Nashville, and the party's leadership, as mentioned, somehow forgot to advance a candidate for the city's district attorney, a position that runs for an incomprehensibly long eight years, making it far more important than the mayor, especially in a time of escalating urban violence. Lately, the DCRP has a new president, Lonnie Spivak, and there is some cause for optimism.

I have increasingly found myself oscillating in the middle of this debate, reluctant to take a public position for personal and professional reasons, while seeing merit in both sides. I have alternatively aligned with the refugee rebels and with the entrenched politicians, sometimes trying to convince the latter to adopt changes advocated by the former. It all felt like a form of schizophrenia—or rather Trumpophrenia, as I initially described it while covering Donald Trump's 2016 campaign for PJ Media. It wasn't long, however, as Trump's policies became clearer, before I became a full supporter of the reformers and the refugees.

Nevertheless, like many, I can still be seduced by politicians. Many of them are charming when you meet them in person, or even when you watch them, primped and prepared, on television. Obviously, that personal appeal is the road to electoral success (though some politicians seem to get by without it). It is not just a matter of telling the people what they want to hear. It is about keeping up an appearance—looking like friend, seeming accessible and easy to talk to. Of course, it's almost completely unlikely you'll actually have a meaningful conversation with a politician, unless you are a mega-donor or someone offering a business deal they can trumpet.

This is, in many ways, the same old same old, apparent to anyone who was even half awake during a rerun of *I, Claudius.* Yet with the United States going through an exceptionally dark period—with virtually every national indicator trending downward, and with federal authorities of questionable integrity and even of evil intent—we need more from our politicians. Considerably more.

Yes, when you go, either singly or collectively, to their offices to seek redress, as the saying goes, many will hear you out. But once the door is shut behind you, it is often the case that you might as well not have bothered to make the effort. I have seen this up close while making the rounds of the Tennessee statehouse with the aforementioned activist Kathleen Harms.

At the same time, when I condemn the politicians, I wonder how I would have fared if I had become a politician myself. Probably, I wouldn't have been so perfect. Like everyone else, or nearly everyone, I have my price. This sense of political realism has allowed me to be more forgiving of individuals when they veer off-road. As a commentator, I hope not to condemn the tottering politicians I know and respect, but rather to nudge them, both personally and in print, in a better direction. I would be journalism's Jiminy Cricket, really, sitting on their shoulders and whispering in their ears.

Sometimes, I imagine that's the role I play with Marsha, though I know that's a pretentious and self-aggrandizing thing to think. She's the senior senator, and I'm just some guy knocking out columns for the *Epoch Times*. In the final analysis, I'd rather be standing in her kitchen sampling the delicious food or beverages she has on offer than telling her what she should or shouldn't be doing. Direct criticisms usually have the effect of making your subject recoil anyway. It's not the way to effectuate change.

Still, I was holding my breath on December 19 and 20, 2022, to see how Blackburn and Bill Hagerty, our Tennessee senators, were going to vote on that staggering $1.7 trillion (with a "t") omnibus spending bill being proffered at the last minute before the GOP took over the House in January 2023. Pushed by Minority Leader Mitch McConnell, this seemed to be no ordinary boondoggle, but rather a bill infused with evil, since it was revealed to include a massive increase for the FBI at a time when that organization's anti-democratic impulses were being made known to the world by Elon Musk and others. This targeted money was meant, in part, to fund the FBI's "efforts to investigate extremist violence and domestic terrorism." Many think the money was actually used to fund government undercover agents. Indeed, the whole January 6, 2021, purported "insurrection" seems to have been a government "false flag" operation with a raft of unanswered questions about the participants. The only person killed was an innocent woman shot at point-blank range by a Capitol Police officer, who was himself later exonerated from any wrongdoing.

And, of course, on the more predictable though nevertheless totally destructive level, this gargantuan spending would add to the already pervasive inflation that had sent our economy into a downward spiral, whether you called what we were experiencing a recession, a depression, or, perhaps more accurately, simply hard times. On top of that, the bill generously funded the mother of all scams—"climate action."

Nevertheless, Senators Marco Rubio and Tom Cotton, of all people, both representing solidly red states (in Rubio's case the most successful red state of all, with the most refugees), were said to be supporting this atrocity of a bill, completely conflicting with the wishes of their voters. Those people wanted an end to the wanton government spending that was impoverishing them—and as rapidly and completely as possible. No doubt the senators' hawkish stance on the Russia–Ukraine war had everything to do with their vote, but they were still extreme disappointments to those skeptics who saw both sides in the conflict as corrupt.

I would include myself among the skeptics, having spent time in the region both during and after the Soviet era, and having smelled the stench of corruption from both quarters everywhere. It was hard to miss. Speaking of pervasive corruption and the attendant deception, it also wasn't long ago that we saw lie after lie in the testimonies of former US officials who were stationed in Ukraine during the impeachment and similar hearings that took place during the Trump presidency. These officials were anxious to tarnish Trump with every brush possible when, in fact, it was Biden who profited from the corruption in Ukraine and Russia, as well as in China and elsewhere. Who could forget him bragging how he was able to muscle the resignation of the man investigating Burisma, the oil company that employed his son for an immense salary, in less than six hours?

And this was all before early May 2023 when, as the *Epoch Times* put it: "The Republican-led House Oversight Committee on May 3 subpoenaed the FBI for a file alleging that a whistleblower linked President Joe Biden to a 'criminal scheme' that involved money for policy decisions while he was the vice president."

Still, I worried how Hagerty and Blackburn would vote. Even though I had considerable confidence in both, I wondered how I would react, personally and politically, should they vote in quisling fashion. I particularly thought of the implications that Marsha's vote had on our cordial relationship. Had I paid my last visit to her kitchen? I didn't want to think someone I liked would support such obviously outrageous legislation, but it had become hard to trust anybody. Those were the times, with tremendous pressure being applied in all directions to everyone, politicians or not, in red states and blue. More and more people were thinking of survival first, seeing the United States as a great nation in serious decline. As I lay in bed at night I found myself thinking once again of the scenes in *Dr. Zhivago* when the doctor's once-beautiful home had been turned by communism into a heart-rending slum, inhabited by multiple impoverished families hunched over living room campfires. Was that to be our fate?

Ultimately, both my senators voted "no" on the dreadful omnibus spending bill that nevertheless passed with the support of eighteen GOP senators, for whom the term "uniparty" might as well have been coined. Fortunately for me, then, I would not have to face the dilemma named by E. M. Forster's oft-quoted adage: "If I had to choose between betraying my country and betraying my friend, I hope I should have the guts to betray my country." Though I'd like to think otherwise, I'm not sure I could be that generous to my friend, any friend really. Well, except for my wife, of course. But she's exactly where I am politically, so it's never been tested. ■

38

FAREWELL, MY PROSTATE

For many, it goes without saying that when you think about moving from one state to another, one of your first considerations is healthcare. Will it be as good as, better than, or worse than in your home state? These days, it's not easy to make that determination since the whole issue has been overwhelmed by the pandemic. We have learned what we should have always known. Every major teaching hospital in the country is bought and paid for to a tremendous extent, and therefore is virtually a slave to the federal government and its medical policies. To put it mildly, those policies don't always coincide with your physical well-being. They can also impair one's mental health.

This goes for red and blue states both. Healthcare is, was, and probably always will be a scarcity, no matter what Klaus Schwab and his Davos cronies tell you during some World Economic Forum speech about how life would be better if there were just fewer people on the planet.

This is especially true of government healthcare. As we have seen in Canada and the UK, socialized medicine does not work—it will always be rationed. But neither does free market medicine (though it is somewhat better), unless you are among the rich or are willing and able to pay extra to a concierge doctor or the equivalent. This was an inescapable truth for the refugees, many of whom tell me they are still searching for the right doctor, as it is for everybody else. It's been that way for a long time. COVID just exposed the situation to light.

Recently, the functional medicine movement—a holistic approach combining Eastern and Western methods—has been making some inroads into this highly frustrating problem. It promises to be cheaper too. But as useful as it may prove to be, it will only take us so far. At some point you are likely to find yourself on the operating table with impossibly bright lights shining on you, an anesthetist about to put you under more quickly than you can imagine while the surgeon sits hunched at a computer terminal, poised to trigger a robot that will cut you open with a precision, we are told, no human could match.

I should have known better, but I didn't consider any of this in great detail before my family and I made our decision for Nashville and vicinity. It probably wouldn't have mattered anyway. I was reassured by the presence of the Vanderbilt University Hospital, highly rated by *U.S. News*'s Hospital Rankings, not that I really trusted that media company. Their college rankings barely ever changed. How is that possible?

But Vanderbilt was rated particularly highly in urology, an area where I long had had a problem. Seven years before, I had been diagnosed with prostate cancer. It was shocking at first. I can remember walking down LA's Third Street past Cedars-Sinai Medical Center in a daze. Was this the end, so soon? I hadn't yet written my own version of Raymond Chandler's *Farewell, My Lovely*, or anything near that good.

I was reassured, to the extent possible, that the cancer was probably slow-growing. According to the rather complicated scoring system that is supposed to tell you the level of disease in the various sections of the prostate gland, my cancer was Gleason 6 (3+3). Six is on the low end. So I went and stayed for a long time on what they call "active surveillance," having a couple of rather painful biopsies along the way that gave reassuring results. My PSA (prostate-specific antigen) was simultaneously monitored, although this was said to be a less accurate gauge, sometimes relied upon and sometimes discarded.

Nevertheless, a jump in my PSA to around 11 sent me in for another biopsy to discover my Gleason score had gone up to 8, in the danger zone. Alarm bells went off—it was time for action.

This is where my personal health issues oddly intersected in an extremely unnerving way with what must be, with the possible exception of the COVID pandemic, the most controversial health-care issue of our times: transgender surgeries, often for children, and their handmaiden, hormone therapy.

As it happened, Vanderbilt University Hospital was at the center of this controversy, especially after Matt Walsh released his afore-mentioned documentary, *What Is a Woman?*. The film generated an outcry from conservative and libertarian journalists and even awakened some normally somnolent Tennessee Republican politi-cians who suddenly were making noises about restrictive legislation.

At nearly the same time, a woman in a key hospital position had been overheard publicly admitting how much money Vanderbilt was and would be making from such surgeries. If you get them young, they will be coming back over a lifetime for lucrative repairs, reversals, or whatever. It was a perpetual assembly line of genital transformation.

Soon enough the embarrassed hospital had no choice but to abandon these practices—tantamount to child abuse at its most extreme—not that they weren't still available in many other parts of the country.

Where did I fit into all this? At my age, sexual reassignment was not exactly at the top of my bucket list. More urgent were items like "going on a safari" or "attending all four tennis Grand Slams" (I had already been to two). Nevertheless, in pursuing my own treatments I found myself uncomfortably and unavoidably close to the healthcare controversy surrounding transgenderism only a few days after my latest biopsy.

From here on, in what became my adventure in modern medicine, I will be referring to the doctors involved as Doctors A and B. This is because I am no expert in prostate treatment beyond what I learned in the line of fire, and because the decisions I took were mine. Others in related medical circumstances may have valid reasons for taking a different route.

Doctor A, whom I knew only slightly even though he had been my urologist for some time, informed me rather peremptorily online and in person, within days of my diagnosis, of the treatment he was recommending. It was to be radiation accompanied by injections of something called Lupron. I had never heard of it, but when he immediately added, during our brief personal meeting, that I would probably only have to take it for two years and could stop after a few months if I really didn't like it, I began to suspect something.

Lupron, I quickly learned, is a testosterone blocker, the same drug, I correctly surmised, they inject in young boys who want to transition to girls. I was starting to get more than a little agitated.

I didn't learn this information from Dr. A, however, who had left the examining room in less than five minutes for another patient, before I had a chance to formulate my questions, let alone ask them. Such is the conveyor-belt quality of much of modern medicine. I had no idea when or if he was coming back.

I learned it from a nurse who entered the room only a few minutes later and handed me a brochure about Lupron from the pharmaceutical company that manufactured it, AbbVie. She also informed me they had scheduled a visit to the radiation oncologist for the next morning. His office was downstairs. After I had seen him, I could come upstairs and get my first Lupron injection right then without having to visit the hospital twice. How convenient.

At that point, I had many questions, but I didn't want to ask them. I wanted to go home and think this through, maybe have a stiff drink. I told the somewhat bewildered nurse to put a pin in all this and I left. One thing I knew: I didn't want any testosterone blockers in my butt.

I had several friends who were doctors or other kinds of healthcare professionals. Very soon I was on the phone with them and subsequently the experts they recommended. Lingering in my brain, however, was something that made me distinctly uncomfortable: the best medicine was practiced in New York, California, or Massachusetts—all blue states—or Texas, which was red but not really so in its medical capital, Houston. What was I doing in Tennessee? I had made a mistake moving from LA. I was irresponsible. I could have been treated at Cedars-Sinai or UCLA, where the doctors were, I was convinced at the time, better. Also on my mind was the repellent Vanderbilt transgenderism scandal. I wanted to be as far from that as possible. (Of course, I wouldn't be farther from it in those blue states. I would actually be in the heart of it.)

Calling around, however, led not back to LA but to New York— to NYU Langone, said to have become the ne plus ultra of healthcare, thanks to some extraordinarily generous donations. I took Zoom calls with two of their obviously illustrious doctors. They examined my biopsy and pathology results and gave their opinions. Each was recommending a slightly different approach. I wasn't sure how to make sense of this. Choices abounded, from a new high-tech process from Israel called alpha radiation to the proton therapy you see advertised on television. That alone made me hesitant. Filtering through these discussions, however, was the name of a surgeon who happened to be back at Vanderbilt—Dr. B. Had I seen him? The New York doctors were surprised I hadn't.

In the company of my wife, I went to see Dr. B. It was obvious within minutes that this was the man. He would do my prostatectomy. This was beneficial in that I would be in my home city for the inevitable follow-up. I wouldn't have to get on a plane to New York or wherever for a doctor's appointment. More importantly, there would be no Lupron or other hormone blocker. I wouldn't be transgendered at seventy-eight.

The catch was I would have to wait. Dr. B was going to Africa, as he frequently did, to operate on people there. He was older and still able to perform prostatectomies the old way, by hand, without robots. The younger doctors only knew the robotic method, but there weren't any robots where Dr. B was going. What did that augur for the future, when he and others like him were too old to do this? Who would replace them in low-tech regions of the world? Dr. B's generosity made me like him all the more. I got on the queue, which meant I would have to wait several months for the operation. He assured me that I wasn't in danger from the delay.

The interim time turned out to be extremely valuable, because it was among the most rewarding periods of my life. When local friends of ours—almost all of whom were evangelicals—heard of my imminent operation, they told me and my wife that they would pray for me. Despite my years in Middle Tennessee, I was still largely a coastal, secular person. I was not used to such pronouncements. I was close to astonished. It's difficult for me to find the words to express how moved I was by this. It seemed they were serious— and indeed they were. I can't remember when I last cried, but this brought tears to my eyes on several occasions, forcing me to look away. I will never forget it.

At the same time, I got a similarly prayerful response from the rabbi at Chabad of Nashville. For a long time, I had realized that if I wished to reconnect with my Judaism, it would be through Chabad, an organization that I had already known for its nonjudgmental outreach to secular Jews and for its noble work fighting substance abuse. Nothing like a little cancer to focus you on the important.

My colleagues at the *Epoch Times* were also deeply supportive and sympathetic, both when we were together and when we were not. Many of them "cultivate," in their words, the Falun Gong movement—a renewed form of Buddhism and Taoism for our times that became immensely popular in China in the 1990s with roughly a hundred million adherents. The movement then became the object of extreme communist repression, including forced organ transplants from its members. This forced a migration of many Falun Gong to America and other countries.

Some of them founded the *Epoch Times* in 2000. I had, some time back, intermittently tried some of their meditative exercises, but I recently felt the desire to know more. As I lay in bed recuperating, I finally read their seminal book, *Zhuan Falun*, from lectures by their leader Hongzhi Li. I didn't understand it all, especially those parts suffused with Chinese cultural history unknown to me, but other parts were remarkably meaningful—even contemporary and compelling. I resolved to know still more.

I was also realizing that there had been a change in my writing, not so much in its wording or style but in its intent. When I was a young novelist/screenwriter, of course I loved literature and movies, but I wrote mostly for egotistical reasons—essentially to show off how clever and creative I was, and maybe to attract the opposite sex. That had morphed, as I was seeing more clearly during this interim period, into a less self-serving goal. Earning fame and fortune was no longer my primary motivation, though some of that would admittedly always be there. What really impelled me to write was the desire to help preserve what was left of our once-great republic. That drove me to the computer every morning without hesitation. I rarely got up except to eat or exercise, and I often ate at my desk. I have never been happier with my chosen profession.

Looking back on this recent period of my life, I feel to a small extent that I was plunged into the fight for medical freedom without realizing it. We refugees have a significant role to play, coming from afar and having to seek out, as nearly everyone does at some point, healthcare for ourselves and our families all over again. It's not hard to see, when you are a newcomer, how many fine doctors—my general practitioner, for example—are trapped by a government-dictated medical system that limits and often disrupts their ability to treat patients. Some of the constraints are obvious, such as those surrounding hydroxychloroquine and ivermectin during height of COVID hysteria; others are more subtle. But they are pervasive.

We can no longer be passive recipients of our healthcare. That's a nostalgic memory from the past out of some long-gone Jimmy Stewart movie, where the avuncular family doctor showed up at your house with his black medical bag to make everything okay and give the kids lollipops. If those days ever return, it will be a miracle. It is incumbent on all of us now to be proactive with our healthcare, even obnoxious if necessary—that is, if we want ourselves and our loved ones to survive. ■

39

CAN THE UNIVERSITY OF TENNESSEE WAKE UP THE "WOKE"?

Many Americans, probably most at this point, believe that we are more divided as a nation than we've been since the Civil War, and that this rupture may not be reparable. I mention this in relation to a new government-sponsored program at the University of Tennessee, Knoxville, that appears to yearn for those halcyon days when we all respected each other enough to compromise on the issues or even just talk civilly.

It's called the Institute of American Civics. Its mission, in its own words, "is to provide a comprehensive civic education for University undergraduates and the state at large, including America's founding principles, the economic and political institutions that maintain American democracy and the basics of civic engagement."

It's hard to argue with that mission statement, unless, like me, you see the wisdom in Robert Conquest's Three Laws of Politics, the second of which is "Any organization not explicitly right-wing sooner or later becomes left-wing."

Note that the university's boilerplate specifies "American democracy," not "American republicanism," which would be more accurate to our Constitution, but that's probably the nitpicking of an apostate who is a former left-winger like Conquest.

The new institute, the product of bipartisan legislation, was created by an overwhelmingly Republican Tennessee Assembly in 2022 to be part of the university's Howard H. Baker Jr. Center for Public Policy, which was itself founded in 2003. Baker was the first Republican senator ever from Tennessee, serving for nearly twenty years from 1967, during which time he had served as both minority and majority leader. Known as the "Great Conciliator," he was famed for maintaining civility and forging compromises.

And if you look at the thirteen-member Board of Fellows selected to guide the new institute, you find a great deal of conciliation going on, starting at the top with the two former Tennessee governors, Phil Bredesen and Bill Haslam. Both Republicans, in today's terms they might easily be accused of being RINOs, but Tennessee at its highest political rungs has long swung to the moderate. It was how the Republicans overcame the Democrats in the first place, by appearing only slightly to the right of them or sometimes not at all.

With the refugees arriving, plus Trump, of course, the situation is different now, but less middle-of-the-road, more ideological voices do appear on the list of fellows, including Princeton's Robert P. George on the right and, on the left, presidential historian Jon Meacham, whose dark and angry speeches for President Biden have been heavily criticized by conservatives.

Seemingly the lone true libertarian among the fellows is UT law professor Glenn Reynolds, who is also known to the public at large as InstaPundit, a.k.a. the Blogfather, for being the first one to popularize the form just after 9/11. (To be accurate, InstaPundit actually went online serendipitously just before September 11, 2001, which accounted for only some of its success. The rest belongs to the brilliant Reynolds.)

I have been a friend of Glenn's for roughly twenty years. In fact, I owe a great deal of my career change to him: InstaPundit inspired me to start a blog of my own, and from there PJ Media, with which Glenn has also been involved. I might not even be writing this book were it not for Glenn. I also may not have moved to Nashville, which I had assumed, cluelessly, to be right around the corner from Knoxville, where he lives. It's a three-hour drive at best, unless you go at three o'clock in the morning.

I was obviously eager to hear his opinion of this latest government undertaking, so I called him via Zoom to chat about it. Was there something of significance here? Could it make an impact? Or was it just another mask for the various forms of leftist propaganda that had been destroying American higher education for years, this time with the imprimatur and cash infusion of a Republican state assembly? Since Glenn and I agree on almost everything, I doubted he would countenance the latter.

Indeed, on the one issue we did once disagree—the central theme of this book, as it happens—I'm pleased to say he now sees eye to eye with me. I don't have to revise everything I've written. Early on, as I've earlier discussed, when Reynolds first noticed the influx of blue staters to Tennessee, he wittily suggested on Insta-Pundit that welcome wagons be set up to explain to these blue-infused interlopers they were in a red state. He now acknowledges that these same interlopers tend to be more conservative than the original residents. He sees them all around him, flowing into Knoxville from California, New York, and Illinois—what he calls "upper-crusty professional people," almost always conservative.

With that minor capitulation, I was more than willing to accept what he said in praise of the new institute, which he insists is really an attack on the woke university through the side door. The objective is not to make the University of Tennessee right-wing, an impossibility anyway, but to nudge it toward the center—to make UT, in essence, what colleges were decades ago: even-handed.

Glenn and UT president Randy Boyd, once a successful entrepreneur, see this as a potential marketing coup for the university, since more and more students and families are looking for college campuses that have not morphed into indoctrination centers reminiscent of the Chinese Cultural Revolution. One extraordinarily wealthy woman, a financier of many conservative causes who moved with her family from New York to Tennessee, is already planning to send her homeschooled children to the University of Tennessee instead of the Ivy League, where they would have been welcomed with open arms (the mother could have donated enough to fund another wing on the medical school or a new football stadium).

Such is the corruption of American higher education. Could the Institute of American Civics fix it? Certainly not by itself, but it could add force to an existing trend. Actual academic even-handedness could be becoming an attraction. Just a few years ago the University of Tennessee had around twenty thousand students. In 2022 it had 33,805. They are aiming for more than fifty thousand, Glenn told me. Princeton University, by comparison, has 8,623.

Princeton, now excessively woke, was once regarded as the Southern Ivy, where the well-heeled of Atlanta and Nashville would go for a proper education. My evidence is still largely anecdotal, but these days the trend seems to be reversing, with Northern families sending their sons and daughter to places like the University of the South in Sewanee so that they can still recognize them when they come home for Thanksgiving.

Unfortunately, the gorgeous Sewanee, where I recently visited, has it problems. But nobody's perfect.

If the new Institute works as envisioned by Boyd and Reynolds, the University of Tennessee, because of its size and its ability to reach all levels of society, has an even greater role to play in returning higher education to its better values. The Institute of American Civics is something for everyone, especially for refugees and their children, to watch. ∎

40

"COUNTRY ON": NEW YEAR'S EVE 2023, NASHVILLE

One of the great personal pleasures of moving from a blue state to a red state is that you can be yourself. But it takes a while for that to fully set in, rather like Elizabeth Kübler-Ross's five stages of grief, but in reverse.

That was true for me. Although I had been publicly outspoken on the radio and in print since I relocated, and for years in Los Angeles as well, I frequently had my back up against the wall when airing my opinions. It wasn't relaxing. Many others remained secretive about their beliefs long after their addresses had changed. Some simply had conflict-averse personalities; others had professional reasons for keeping quiet. I heard about a particularly extreme case, in which a successful entertainment lawyer who was fed up with the stultifying and monolithic culture of California decamped to a one-hundred-acre estate in the upscale rural paradise of Leiper's Fork, not far from Franklin. This lawyer, however, never even told his connections back in Los Angeles that he had moved, for fear it would destroy his business. This was a trick you could pull off only in the internet age—but one wonders how long you could keep it up.

Among the last compulsions to wither away, if it ever does completely, is the need to convince friends and family in your state of origin (ones you may have disappointed or even angered in leaving) that you did the right thing, and that maybe they should even follow you. These are the last people you can influence because it often threatens them the most. It's easier to sway a random person sitting next to you on a plane.

I realized I was beginning to pass through those stages finally as New Year's 2023 approached. Nashville apparently was to be the center of the celebration on national media, supplanting New York, at least for television and probably beyond. CBS and Fox had placed their bets with Music City. More people would be in Times Square—although the 200,000 predicted in downtown Nashville wasn't too shabby—but the entertainment would be coming from red Tennessee's capital city.

A lineup including Jason Aldean, Sheryl Crow, Luke Bryan, Jimmie Allen, Elle King, and Darius Rucker was being touted. Several of those country stars have recently made publicly known their support of our republic and its Constitution. Aldean has done so, in the company of his wife Brittany, who has a heavy presence on social media, as did Bryan in his latest hit, "Country On." The song's lyrics couldn't be clearer—touting that the USA had not seen its better days; praising the farmers, cowboys, firemen, and soldiers that are the backbone of our nation.

The irony, of course, is that Nashville is itself blue. It's blue, however, in a strange way, surrounded by red just miles outside. It was people from these areas who'd be the bulk of the New Year's Eve throng. Being a bit old to brave the crowds (not that we were ever that fond of them), my wife Sheryl and I decided this New Year's to have a small group of friends over for dinner to celebrate—adults who didn't feel it necessary to stay up until the midnight ball dropped (or, now, the musical note that came down in Nashville).

That dinner proved to be the most relaxed and, in an odd way, insightful New Year's I have ever experienced. Among the group was my now-old friend of four years in Nashville, Frank Gorgie, that rarest of birds: a university political science teacher who actually taught the subject and didn't use it for indoctrination. With Gorgie was his wife Jean, also a professor, of English lit. Gigi Levangie and her husband, Chris Elise, were there as well. Gigi is a screenwriter, and she's the author of *The Starter Wife* (which was made into a TV series) and other bestselling novels. Chris is a photographer who specialized in capturing the athletic brilliance of the NBA until the objectively pro-fascist views of LeBron James and company got the better of him. Chris also happened to be a black guy with an Afro whose politics since childhood tilted conservative. He was French by birth and upbringing, but he was now an American citizen by choice.

All six of us were former Los Angelenos with no intention of going back. Thus, we shared certain memories. Several of us were also once left-leaning to one degree or another. What made the evening special was that we could all say what we wanted, about anything, without any impulse to self-censor. That meant we could criticize other conservatives as well. Nobody's perfect, to say the least. On this evening, we were never watching our backs in any way, something that had become reflexive for most of us.

We jabbered on and on about just about everything under the sun, largely focusing on what others had done and what we could do to revive this once unique and magnificent nation of ours. Without us realizing it, it was a cathartic experience. Call it the great shedding. You could breathe free, as Emma Lazarus once said of our country. It was still possible. All you had to do was do it. Gatherings like this were essentially political acts, while also being the most enjoyable and seemingly innocuous of social events. They constituted the last of those reverse Kübler-Ross stages.

As the evening wore on, both at home and, via the television screen, at the festivities going on downtown until the small hours of the morning, it became clearer (not that it hadn't been for some time) that conservatives were now the cool kids, and that liberals and progressives were what we used to call the squares. The world had flipped. And freedom of speech was at the core of it. Only the squarest of square could profess to be hip while suppressing the thoughts and beliefs of others. Obviously, this is cowardly, not hip—and utterly conformist. More importantly, it leads, in subtle and unsubtle ways, to a new form of totalitarianism that must be opposed at every turn. A nation of sheep was being built, far too many of whom were among the young.

Glenn Greenwald, an independent journalist and a sometime- (maybe I should say former-) leftie, clarified the ominous results of this trend on his Substack:

> Far more alarming, far more alarming, is the support that this authoritarian censorship scheme is given by the vast majority of followers of the Democratic Party. And the reason for their support is as toxic as it is easily proven establishment left liberals are now among the millions of new Americans who simply no longer believe in free speech as a reflexive, foundational, defining American value. They do not want free speech to exist. They are against it. Unlike that consensus I celebrated back in 2006, modern-day liberals want the government to unite with corporate power to deny basic free speech rights to their political adversaries, and to know that you don't need to listen to me but to them.

Despite Greenwald's grim diagnosis, for New Year's Eve in Nashville and environs, the party played on in the streets and private homes. Freedom was still in the air. But as Ben Franklin wondered for our republic more generally, can we keep it?

ADDENDUM: With great sorrow, I must report that one of our dinner party, Chris Elise—tall, lean, and fit in his fifties—died tragically in his sleep just before this book went to print. To say this magnificent man "will be missed" is a cliché and in this case an understatement. RIP, Chris Elise. ∎

41

STEEPLES: HOW THE SOUTH
GAVE ME RELIGION

One of the first things I noticed about Tennessee when I moved to the state in June 2018 was the prevalence of steeples, and thus churches. They were seemingly everywhere, on every corner.

I wasn't used to that. When you live in California and are largely secular, inadvertently you find yourself ignoring the existence of religious institutions, though of course there are many famous ones in the giant state, like the Crystal Cathedral in Garden Grove. Nevertheless, such edifices, even magnificent ones, have a tendency to fade into the woodwork against the ever-multiplying stimuli of the environment vying for your attention, high-tech and otherwise. And despite efforts to popularize digital worship, only a small few look to their cell phones and iPads for any kind of genuine relationship with God when Tinder and the like are only a few clicks away.

Not that this meant much to me. I was too busy with my life and the object of true worship for most Angelenos of my ilk: my career. I was comfortable in my agnostic and vague "there's something out there" beliefs. The creation of the universe was beyond my pay grade, I would joke to those interested, and there weren't many who were. Anyway, I was busy with the mundane.

On some occasions, however, I would stop to think, as when a member of the Chabad school of Hasidic Judaism would accost me on the sidewalk and ask if I were Jewish. When I responded positively, he would ask if I would like to put a phylactery box on my forehead—that reminder Jews have to keep the law—and pray that day. I usually demurred, though once in a while—out of curiosity or guilt—I might go forward with the request. Other times, almost always around the High Holy Days, I would suddenly wish I were a member of a congregation and would end up attending services given by talk show host Dennis Prager—not an ordained rabbi but more knowledgeable than almost all who were—because I knew him from having appeared on his radio show to talk politics or promote my books. Neither were spiritual acts. And Prager's shul, such as it was, was only opened for the Jewish New Year and Day of Atonement. The rest of the year I rarely entered a synagogue, or any other religious institution, for that matter.

But when I arrived in Nashville, I kept noticing those steeples, especially in the southern, more suburban part of Davidson County where I lived. They spilled into the neighboring counties as well, and into the state beyond, as I would find out not long thereafter. I didn't pay too much heed at first—I was still figuring out how to get from here to there by myself in my eagerness not to rely on a GPS. But just a few weeks after my move, my attention was turned in a more spiritual direction in a surprising venue. At the gym, I ran into a man to whose home I had been invited only a few days before to meet a candidate for local office. The man greeted me warmly and, seemingly automatically, asked me, as a newcomer, what church I would be joining. For a split second I wondered if he were soliciting for his own, but when I explained I was Jewish he seemed surprised for his own split second. Then he asked, well, what synagogue was I joining—as if, of course, I would join one. That was, the obvious subtext implied, what everyone did hereabouts. Our identities, both spiritual and social, came from our place of worship.

I hadn't given it much more than a passing thought, though I did soon learn there were five synagogues in Metro Nashville. Eventually, my wife and I visited them all, dutifully but somewhat halfheartedly, unable to commit to any. Part of it was the same problem we, and many more moderate Jews, had in Los Angeles and elsewhere. Jewish congregations were too mired in trendy social justice ideology that ironically ran in contradistinction to the religion itself. It was an old story I easily recognized from the radicalism of my own youth: the need to avoid discrimination by abandoning one's religion that led many Jews to adopt atheistic communism. That didn't work, as the demise, by assassination and other means, of Trotsky and other Jews in Stalin's politburo would soon attest. But the dream of escape through secularism lived on through the generations, a bad self-destructive habit that was extremely difficult to shake, weirdly akin to smoking.

I later heard from my *Epoch Times* colleague Trevor Loudon that too many Christian churches had gone in the same direction. But what would be the result for me? I didn't smoke, at least not the deadly smoke of socialism. Was I to spend my life an alienated modern man, far from God, a slave of my own ambitions?

I don't know if other refugees had these thoughts—some may have; I never asked because it felt too private—but I definitely did, even if only in the back of my mind, when I first moved to Tennessee. Would this journey have a spiritual impact on me? And, indeed, something had seemed to change in my thoughts on spirituality, beginning in the early days of our move.

Around the same time, I met a man named Langley Granbery, who probably does not realize what a profound influence he has had on me. Langley, with Frank Gorgie, was one of the men who sought me out when I first moved. This was flattering, of course, and our families became close over the years. Langley and I don't see each other that often, about once a month for lunch, primarily at the local Whole Foods. Langley liked that Whole Foods because it was part of a shopping mall owned by his family. He was from one of the old real estate families that had built the city, but you wouldn't know it from how he comported himself. He was humble to a degree that could be unnerving, especially to me when we first met, after I had freshly arrived from the city that could be called the world's capital of ego.

Langley was also the first friend I had made whose character was imbued with deeply held Christian beliefs. Those beliefs permeated him in a way that is difficult for me to explain, but they came from a paradoxically self-assured diffidence I had never encountered. He would give me Christian literature; again, for a split second I wondered if he was trying to convert me, though I almost immediately realized that wasn't his intention. He wanted me to understand, to see the importance of faith in the greater sense, and I am grateful to him for that, because, to some small degree, it worked. When he knew I was going for my prostate operation, he gave me a tiny edition of the Christian gospels.

But faith for me did not mean Christianity—much as I admired and often sought to emulate, fitfully, the teachings of Christ. Instead it meant a return to, or perhaps more accurately a renewal of, my Judaism. I suspect Langley would be glad to hear he inspired that. It came through taking the first small steps to attending, in person or via Zoom, the local Chabad, which has a strong presence in Nashville under Rabbi Yitzchok Tiechtel. This rabbi has done an enviable job of staying apolitical in trying times while making a comfortable and welcoming home for those estranged from other Jewish institutions because of the often-overweening ideological bias. He also has a sly sense of humor.

So, as a refugee, I am the servant of two spiritual masters, Judaism and Falun Gong, trying to balance and make sense of them, when previously I had none. In an attempt to reconcile Falun Gong and Judaism, I buttonholed Cindy Drukier—an *Epoch Times* senior producer of Jewish background who I knew cultivated Falun Gong but had a scientist brother deeply involved with Chabad—and asked how she dealt with this dichotomy. Did she practice both? She didn't, but she found basic similarities between the two in spiritual discussions with her brother. They connected on that level, if not on the particulars of their disciplines.

That was interesting, and in a way reassuring, but didn't resolve things for me. I don't know how or if I will do so in the future. I do know my migration awakened something. But as previously noted, in this I may be unique among the refugees. Most others I have spoken with were already quite religious before they came. Their convictions were a great part of their motivation. They wanted to be among the faithful—and they are.

This religious motivation was made clear to me literally the day after I wrote the previous part of this chapter. After procrastinating for a time, I had finally made arrangements to drive down to Westhaven again for a meeting of refugees that occurred Friday mornings at a place called Scout's Pub. I expected perhaps a dozen people in a back room and was surprised to find the entire establishment filled to capacity with close to a hundred people. All were men, mostly on the senior side of sixty but a few younger. A few were there for the first time—they raised their hands when asked, I among them—and the rest were regulars. Many, it turned out, were migrants from blue states, some recent, others from as long as five or six years ago.

Since the burning political issue of the moment was the increasingly bloody battle for Speaker currently going on in the House, with the vote count then at eleven and mounting, I expected that to be the major topic of discussion. Indeed, that was my primary reason for going there on this day—to get their views on the subject and report on them. I was wrong. The subject of discussion that morning—as it was, I learned, every Friday—was God.

The man who led that discussion and convened the weekly gathering was Steve Doan, a retired basketball coach from Northern California and a garrulous fellow who spoke in a manner somewhere between a Southern preacher and a coach exhorting his players during a huddle. He told the group a historical story reminiscent of the *Titanic* disaster—I didn't quite get its provenance—of some young seamen who, despite the urgings of their captain to save themselves, remained true to the principles of what, Doan insisted, it meant to be a man and went down with their vessel, allowing the women and children to survive in the few dinghies.

Doan prefers to avoid the hurly-burly of politics for his gatherings. As he informed me, the overall message he delivers to the group every week was that "God loves you." Whatever one's problems, be they personal, financial, or political, accepting the reality of divine love was the most important step in solving them.

What further surprised me was that Doan was far from the only sports person in the room. The pub was filled with them— ex-players and coaches, some quite well known from the National Football League and the National Basketball Association. Despite their age, they could have put up a good team if pressed. I spoke for a bit with Rich Garza, who had been the chaplain for the San Antonio Spurs and, prior to that, a lineman in the NFL. We reminisced about the sad destruction of the once most beautiful place on earth, California, a state he knew well from the multi-year rivalry between the Spurs and my former home team, the Los Angeles Lakers. He also bemoaned, more politely than I, the descent into wokeness of the brilliant Spurs coach Gregg Popovich, a friend of his of many years.

I mentioned the prevalence of retired athletes and coaches to realtor Dave Markowicz, who had urged me to come to these gatherings and had just debuted his website to help families considering migration to "find freedom." He pointed out what I should have realized after my years in Tennessee. Many of these men originally were Southerners, from regions where sports play a significant role in the daily lives of citizens. They had then roamed the globe in pursuit of their athletic careers, put down roots in various locations, even some foreign countries, where their team assignments took them, only to return to the South years later. The South, and red states generally, had become the place to be for patriots. A number of these men had become surprisingly cosmopolitan, having carried with them all kinds of new experiences while maintaining, above all, their faith. Were they, then, refugees? Maybe they were returnee refugees, having come back home to a place some never thought they would, to live among friends and to rebuild our country. ■

42

ON THE CUSP OF THE NEW

The aforementioned struggle of the twenty Republican congressmen and congresswomen to exact serious reforms in the way the United States Congress conducts its business, in exchange for electing Kevin McCarthy Speaker, promised to remake American politics in 2023. There were many possible ramifications, including—though on a distinctly smaller level—for my wife and me, as we had instigated the debate that helped propel Andy Ogles, one of the twenty, into office. Sheryl and I were unlikely to have been involved in anything of this potentially historical significance had we not become refugees from California to Tennessee four years before.

Ogles, as a freshman, had joined the twenty early on by affiliating with the Freedom Caucus weeks before traveling to Washington to serve. He soon found himself in the middle of something that the Left and the media chose (for obvious political purposes) to call "chaos," but which was in reality the unruly democratic process in action.

I availed myself of my connection to Ogles to get an inside view of the negotiations as they were happening, which I wrote up in a late-night article for the *Epoch Times* that went viral, with thousands of downloads. This redounded well to Ogles, who became one of the better known of the twenty, surprisingly so for a freshman. This may ultimately make him more of a force in future Tennessee politics than others might've anticipated. Tennessee Republicans at the higher levels tend to be risk averse. Ogles had shown himself not to be. Most of the refugees applauded this attitude, making him a new kind of leader should he continue on the same path. It will be interesting to see how so-called entrenched elites in Tennessee and in some other red states will respond to the challenge posed by such reformist newcomers: if they will retreat into their shells as if nothing has happened, or if they will themselves reform and respond more directly to their constituents.

Of course, this was all before Ogles's difficulties, mentioned earlier, emerged. Nevertheless, the article made me feel like a small participant in history, if only from a distance. I owe that to my refugee status as well. Judging from the many comments—not always a reliable indication but the one most readily at hand—the reaction to the victory of the twenty was good, yet many were suspicious. Would the Republicans follow through? Was this just another congressional charade, all talk with ultimately no action? The recent Congressional reform was a kind of Rorschach test, dividing optimistic and pessimistic personality types. Buried in these thousands of comments was an interesting pattern. Many of the more optimistic commenters referenced their often-recent moves to red states and how much better they felt having done so. None of the pessimistic commenters, that I can recall, did so.

That made me think about those who move and those who don't and what it means beyond the political. Many people, some of whom I have talked to about it, have considered moving for years, and have asked themselves: Should I go to Florida? Should I go to Tennessee? What about Texas, or even Henderson, Nevada? The latter wouldn't be that far from LA. Yet with certain people, you know early on in these discussions that they are never going to do it. Someone's sick. There's a job. Relatives would disapprove. An excuse crops up. It's always going to be next year, or the year after that. I have empathy for those people, because in reality they should not move. They are not natural refugees. It's not in their personalities. They are like the Italians who remained in Italy during the great migrations, and there's nothing wrong with that. Who doesn't love to visit Italy? And maybe they will be the people who will finally bring needed change to the places, like New York, California, and Illinois, that the rest of us have fled.

Refugees are different kinds of people. To them, the ability to "move on" is part of their DNA. They are people for whom looking for new horizons is a natural, almost instinctive, part of life. Standing still, for them, is moving backward. Not that they become entirely new people. I love country music, but I will never be a real redneck. I still sport a fedora, not a Stetson. Something of the old remains with us. When I contacted Karol Markowicz after many years for this book, I joked with her I could still be reached at my old Los Angeles telephone number. She responded she would take her New York number to her grave. Does that make her a faux Floridian? Of course not—no more than a 323 area code makes me a fake Tennessean. These days, given the endless stream of newcomers, the strange first three digits in our phone numbers cause no shock. Too many people have them.

And now, as if by magic—announced January 10, 2023, by Governor Bill Lee, who was eager to outdo Florida's DeSantis for once—the best of what remains of California is coming to Tennessee: In-N-Out Burger. It will start in Franklin, which will be the eastern hub of the organization, as it spreads across the Nashville area and then nationally. Said Lee: "Tennessee's unmatched business climate, skilled workforce and central location make our state the ideal place for this family-run company to establish its first eastern United States hub. We thank In-N-Out for planting roots in Williamson County and creating new jobs for Tennesseans."

The company's owner and president echoed the sentiments. Now if they'll only do something about their soggy french fries.

Far more important, certainly more important than hamburgers, is that moving keeps you young. It opens those fresh horizons, forging new pathways and connections in your brain in a manner not dissimilar to learning a foreign language (which many of the original refugees to our country obviously had to do) or even to learning something as mundane, but actually deceptively difficult, as operating a computer mouse with your opposite hand. These actions, great and small, pay off in the end. There's a lot to be said for continually challenging yourself. As tennis fans know, Uncle Toni Nadal forced the young Rafael, a natural righty, to learn to play tennis with his left hand. Nadal ended up with what many regard as the greatest forehand in the history of the sport. Few, if any, end up like Nadal, but most of the refugees report being stronger morally, intellectually, and often even physically for having undertaken their journey. I have yet to meet one who wants to go back. ■

43

THE BANALITY OF NO EVIL

Sometimes, as the man said, a cigar is just a cigar.

When I first started writing this book, Metro Nashville, the conservative population anyway, was all aflutter about the sudden and mysterious demise, in his early sixties, of a man named Tim Skow. For some thirty years, Skow hosted a monthly Republican gathering called First Tuesday, to which roughly a hundred people would show up to eat lunch while hearing speeches from various worthies on their side of the aisle, from politicians, even the governor, to media types. Tim—one of the first people I met in Nashville—then struck me as an engaging fellow but curiously lonely for someone who spent so much time organizing people. Maybe, in retrospect, that wasn't so curious. Then one day he plunged to his death from the top of the stairs in his home. Did he fall or was he pushed? Was this an episode out of *House of Cards*, or something more banal, an instance of drinking too much and slipping by accident? Did he have enemies I didn't know about? Was this the dark side of Southern politics that we know from Faulkner and Robert Penn Warren?

I recalled that when I would meet Skow on late afternoons at a watering hole in the Green Hills neighborhood, he was almost always ahead of me, perched at the bar on his second (or was it his third?) drink. This was the kind of man that was easily prey to a Mickey Finn, I recall thinking. Such things happened. Another friend of mine described how he experienced something similar while on a business trip to Arkansas. He ended up without his wallet, license, credit cards, cell phone, and car keys, but he, a former athlete with a substantial presence, was able to track down the villains and retrieve it all, simultaneously enabling the police to break up a gang that was apparently doing this regularly.

It was a better story than Skow's, to which I alluded in an early chapter, hoping a real mystery had transpired and that there would be revelations to add a certain frisson to my book, a bit of Southern Gothic perhaps that would augment my observations with dramatic excitement. No such revelations occurred. Skow's wallet was in his pocket, undisturbed, as was everything else in his house. As for political enemies, they haven't surfaced, though in this town (in every town actually), most people have some. Nevertheless, he probably did fall down the stairs from a surfeit of alcohol—hence Freud's famous quote about cigars. First Tuesday lives on, though it is not the same without Skow, whose contribution to Tennessee has been memorialized by Senator Mark Pody in Senate Joint Resolution 1153, "in memory of Timothy David Skow of Nashville." Skow was a refugee himself, from Spokane, Washington, but some years ago. ■

44

LUNCH WITH ROCKY TOP IN CHANGING TIMES

Minnesota lost nearly twenty thousand residents in 2020, the highest number in at least three decades, according to the Center of the American Experiment, a think tank based in the state. In an interview with *Liz Collin Reports*, three women refugees—to Arizona, Florida, and Texas, respectively—all cited lack of safety and the prevalent disrespect for police as their prime motivation for leaving. How many of the twenty thousand were motivated by the same concerns? Likely a fair percentage, considering the havoc that made Minneapolis virtually unlivable after the George Floyd murder. It was one thing to think that Floyd was the victim of obviously excessive force from white and black policemen, another to use his case as an excuse to destroy a city and leave its citizens defenseless.

I read this (by now common) announcement by these women against a background of rather titanic events occurring in the country that threatened, if anything, to increase the blue-to-red migration. The release over several weeks through independent journalists of the Twitter Files by Elon Musk, the new owner of the social media company, ratified the worst of what many on the right had believed for years: "All the conspiracy theories are true

208 | AMERICAN REFUGEES

so far," wrote Musk. That meant, of course, that numerous Democratic politicians and journalists were stone-cold liars and, worse, that major arms of our government (namely, the Department of Justice and the intelligence agencies) were thoroughly corrupt. Free speech, medical safety, and routine citizens' safety had been shut down by an evil cabal of government and its high-tech partners at Twitter, Facebook, and who knows where else.

Did this mean the refugees were validated in their decision to move and in their proximate activism in their new homes? I didn't even have to ask them. I saw their responses on numerous chat boards, including the "Patriots" board of Chuck Pierce's group, where I found a cartoon of Musk giving the boot to that enemy of public safety George Soros with the legend "Billionaire simps fuck off!" Another cartoon of a short kid socking a bigger opponent in the jaw had this accompanying text: "Never fight until you have to. But when it's time to fight, you fight like you're the third monkey on the ramp to Noah's Ark...and brother, it's startin' to rain."

This last was posted by a guy I knew to have been in Tennessee for less than two years. You could see that it was really starting to rain when another shoe dropped. Joe Biden, our president, had top-secret documents stashed—whether accidentally or on purpose was unknown—in his garage, everywhere but the actual trunk of his treasured 1967 Corvette, although a fair number were stacked willy-nilly no more than ten feet away. Some of those secret documents, incredible as it seems, derived from when Biden was only a senator, making his possession of them in that place totally illegal.

The news of this more than casual disrespect for our nation's security—How many people had rummaged around that garage and at whose behest?—came only after it was first announced that similar documents were found at a place few really knew about, called the Penn Biden Center for Diplomacy & Global Engagement. The latter part presumably meant engagement with communist China, since that country's donations to this "center" ran to the tens of millions, possibly more when you added up the emoluments, many of which went to Biden family members. For what? Well, it was too easy—and truly disheartening if you had the slightest belief in freedom—to guess.

Biden's personal lawyers were in the middle of this, permitted by the Department of Justice to do their own discovery of these documents, at least for a while, until the "optics" were deemed too negative. That was the same DOJ that sent its FBI thugs to break into Trump's Mar-a-Lago at five in the morning.

"It's worse than Watergate," Rocky Top told me. We were having lunch in the Sportsman's Grill, a retro place in Cool Springs, outside Franklin. "Way worse." He would have known, since his political career in Washington began just weeks after that scandal was resolved with Richard Nixon stepping down. "I knew because I watched that press conference to the end...I never do that anymore. Too predictable. But this time they turned on a dime, clamoring in unison, as if taking orders."

He was referring to the press conference when not just Fox's Peter Doocy but the entire legacy media were grilling the hapless Karine Jean-Pierre as if she were an inmate in an Iranian prison. This was the same media that normally formed a firewall around anything that might hurt Biden, even promoting the obvious whopper that son Hunter's laptop was Russian disinformation.

Rocky Top opined that the lockstep media had all gotten phone calls virtually at the same time from their usual sources—Democratic Party functionaries, FBI, CIA, and their editors—that the game had switched. The time to abandon Biden had finally come after all these years—despite the lifetime of lies and plagiarisms, augmented by the rapid decline in the inflationary US economy, the Afghanistan debacle, and the sabotage of our energy independence via the (at this point comical) global warming charade, not to mention the wrecking of our educational system via critical race theory and similar repellent propaganda from kindergarten onward.

At least moral people hoped so. Basic morality was the dividing line.

The doddering, seemingly non compos mentis president was now more a liability than an asset, and it would only get worse were he to run again. He had to be stopped before he formally declared for reelection. Yet Biden still decided to run. What would happen? He had a good chance of losing to Trump (for a second time?) and DeSantis as well. A lot of people, Rocky noted, were in danger of losing their jobs, including a serious number among the deep state as well as their media protectors.

Hence the classified document story was leaked to an array of CBS reporters who claimed to have two sources, and out came the knives. The question, Rocky Top asked, was who is being positioned to replace him in 2024. The Democrat bench (Buttigieg, Klobuchar, and, worst of all, VP Harris) was hopeless. There was California governor Gavin Newsom and a name we both dreaded, because we were afraid she could win: Michelle Obama. Rocky Top felt anyone who attacked her would immediately be silenced by accusations of both racism and sexism. That sounded like our media to me. We both hoped she wouldn't run.

And maybe she wouldn't. Her Achilles' heel was her husband. Who knew how much he would be implicated in the investigations to come? Barack Obama himself told us he wanted to govern from the basement while someone else took the heat. Was he part of, more likely the leader of, the cabal that had put Biden finally in the crosshairs, where he had deserved to be years ago? And if so, might he have helped set off a chain reaction that would tarnish his own reputation in a way he too deserved?

We sat there eating, going on to desserts with no wives present to stop us, in a more optimistic mood than the foregoing might indicate. A dam was breaking, and we both sensed things would never be exactly the same. This was more than Watergate because it spoke directly to the fabric of our nation. It wasn't just about an election that was already won. Where this was all going, we knew not—at least I didn't—but a greater portion of the country was being made aware of a cancer that had overtaken our republic. How they would respond was still a mystery. Would Republican establishment politicians—in Tennessee and across the red states—realize that the ground was shifting and that it was the time to do the people's business rather than business as usual?

Uniformity was unlikely, and not always desirable—an obvious example being the politburo-like behavior of Democrats in Congress—but cause for optimism comes from the fight and victory of those twenty Republicans who withheld their support of Kevin McCarthy as Speaker until the rules of the House were thoroughly rewritten.

It couldn't have happened at a better time, and it was reminiscent of that short kid in the aforementioned cartoon, socking the bully in the mouth. They did it.

The question was how to replicate this victory on the local level, where the refugees were engaged in a fight of their own.

All this happened before Robert F. Kennedy Jr. announced for the nomination in the Democratic Party with policies that harkened to the old "Kennedy" days of his party and more resembled Trump's or even Vivek Ramaswamy's than they did Biden's.

At play was RFK Jr's copiously researched best-seller "The Real Anthony Fauci" that made a mockery of "Slow Joe's" fealty to the doctor's ever-changing pronouncements with all the destruction to American (and global) life that that resulted from them.

The Democratic National Committee's reaction to Kennedy's throwing his hat in the ring was immediate. There would be no primary debates. ■

45

THE MAKINGS OF A
WANNABE REDNECK

In an earlier chapter, I channeled the late Oscar Hammerstein from *Oklahoma!* and asked why the farmers and the cowboys (establishment politicians and refugees) couldn't be friends. But it has suddenly become more urgent. Those establishment politicians, particularly those in red states, had better wake up to their constituents, both refugees and longtime residents, in a changing world. The ground has shifted dramatically.

Jeffrey Tucker of the Brownstone Institute explained it as something we never wanted to believe but now see is true. To an extraordinary extent we are "ruled by liars" and, as of this writing, we haven't heard close to the full story yet.

New Twitter owner and mega-entrepreneur Elon Musk said much the same when he stated, as I excerpted earlier, in a December 24, 2022, interview: "To be totally frank, almost every conspiracy theory that people had about Twitter turned out to be true. Is there a conspiracy theory about Twitter that didn't turn out to be true? So far, they've all turned out to be true. If not more true than people thought."

Do we dare call them conspiracies anymore? Why not allegations to be explored? Or simply…the truth?

But we can't do that—or can we? That would make someone like the much-reviled Representative Matt Gaetz right all along. I admit I often thought the young congressman from Florida's First District had gone too far, that he was the self-aggrandizing extremist the media constantly portrayed him to be as he postured on TV. Sometimes I, too, recoiled, thinking he was hurting the cause, not helping it. But as he demonstrated during the struggle over the speakership, Gaetz, refusing to cave to that rapacious media, was a man of courage and honor. So were his nineteen allies in protest. They may even have converted Speaker Kevin McCarthy into one of their own. These days he seems to be acting that way, ejecting the execrable Adam Schiff and Eric Swalwell from the House Intelligence Committee.

But that hasn't deterred the usual suspects who seek to control us while pretending to support equality (or should I say "equity") while enriching themselves beyond comprehension.

As I conclude this book, the annual meeting of the World Economic Forum in Davos, Switzerland, is taking place. According to news reports, this year's operative word in their ever-changing lexicon is "polycrisis." *Time* magazine describes the term as "the simultaneous and overlapping crises facing the world today: a health crisis, a mounting climate crisis, a war in Europe, an inflation shock, democratic dysfunction, and much more."

I'm particularly amused by the "much more," as if they were advertising a week at an all-inclusive resort, not Klaus Schwab's neo-Marxist "You will own nothing and be happy" proposal for the Great Reset. The globalist's intention, obviously, is never to let a good polycrisis go to waste.

I think we've heard this someplace before. Here in the red states most of us are not buying it. Governor DeSantis spoke for many when he said: "You have a handful of people in Davos deciding all this, that this is how we're supposed to live? Not on my watch. Not here in the state of Florida."

Eighteen other Republican state attorneys general have already joined with Florida to send a letter to Laurence Fink—CEO of BlackRock, Inc., the world's largest asset managing firm to the tune of $10 trillion in investments—protesting the company's adherence to the exclusionary ESG policies that obsess the Davos crowd.

I am disappointed that Tennessee governor Bill Lee has thus far been silent on this issue, considering the threat BlackRock and other globalists are to the many small businesses that make up the heart and soul of his state.

But no matter. I have decided not to allow a few retrograde politicians to disturb my enjoyment of life in the great free state of Tennessee. We all have to accommodate to where we live at some level. In a way, it's a positive compromise from which one can grow. And besides, since I haven't yet met a single refugee who returned to his state of origin, I don't want to be the first.

Further, I'm happier than I have ever been in Tennessee and grateful for the wonderful people I have met here, many of whom have been described in this book. Notably missing are perhaps the best of all—the plumbers, electricians, HVAC folks, construction workers, and the like who, when I have talked to them, have exhibited more common sense and more down-home patriotism for this country than any group of people I have ever met.

So, come Indian summer, or whenever you are reading this book, you might find me driving my aging convertible south on the Hillsboro Pike toward Franklin, Luke Bryan blaring from the Big 98, the major country music station hereabouts. Or even further out on the Minnie Pearl Memorial Highway in Centerville, though you won't hear me let out any "Hee-haws" or "How-DEEEEES!" like Minnie did in her trademark holler at the Grand Ole Opry.

Nevertheless, if it's a sunny day and you look very closely, you might see a hint of red beginning to appear on the back of my neck. Such things happen—even to native New Yorkers. ∎

EPILOGUE

NASHVILLE TAKES A DARK TURN

Some weeks after this book was finished, but soon enough to be able to append this brief description, a horrifying event occurred on April 3, 2023, in Nashville, not far from where I live.

Six people—including three nine-year-old students—were murdered in a small Christian school called Covenant. The killer was a twenty-eight-year-old woman named Audrey Hale, a onetime student at the school herself, who in recent years "presented," in modern parlance, as a man—so much so that she was dressed in faux military garb, complete with a red bandana covering her hair, and armed with an array of weaponry, when she did her maximally evil deed.

The city justifiably went into something approximating shock. It seemed everyone knew someone who was connected to the murdered children in some way. But as is so often the case in today's America, the event was almost instantaneously politicized, locally and nationally, before the children's parents and the community at large could even begin to grieve.

It was seized upon by two members of the state assembly, young black men who had recently morphed into radicals (one with a beachball-sized Afro), looking and acting like wannabe Brooklyn-era Al Sharptons, or Huey P. Newtons. Not long before in college, however, the same guys, both named Justin, were the picture of preppy bourgeois propriety in jacket and tie, one of them running for president of Bowdoin on a platform of bringing Republicans and Democrats together in 2016.

Evidently, Justin Jones and Justin J. Pearson had seen an advantage in changing their style. In the wake of the killings, they wrangled, with the help of mostly anonymous wealthy George Soros–types providing buses and so forth, several hundred more-or-less clueless high school students from in and out of state—many of whom were themselves transgender—to demonstrate in front of and attempt to stampede inside the Tennessee State House for that mightiest of all causes without proof of efficacy: gun control.

The two young assemblymen entered the building ahead of the (mostly) teenaged students and, standing in the well of the House to which they had been recently elected by astonishingly few voters (fewer than five hundred in one case), only feet from the Speaker, employed a bullhorn. They exhorted the students to enter and demanded immediate action from the assemblymen and assemblywomen in a manner that had never been seen before in the history of the Tennessee State House and was obviously 100 percent against the rules of virtually any legislative body.

A day later they were expelled. But their fellow traveler in the assembly, a white woman leftist named Gloria Johnson, had escaped expulsion by one vote because she had not employed the bullhorn.

This decision to keep Johnson turned out to be a drastic mistake, because she—by far the worst of the three and the most hypocritical—walked outside and told reporters the reason she had not been expelled was that her colleagues were racist. They had favored her whiteness.

This was a complete lie, but like many such lies it made its way across the country in minutes to dominate cable news for several days.

The assembly and its Speaker didn't have the courage to stand by their original decision. The two Justins were taken back just days later to work alongside their white female compatriot.

Meanwhile, lost in the predictable fodder for CNN et al. were unanswered questions about the killings. Who was the shooter, Audrey Hale, anyway? Why did she do it? She had left a "manifesto," as well as other documents. What was in all of them? Had she become anti-Christian? Was she taking hormone therapy, testosterone, to aid her female-to-male transition? Might that have contributed to or even instigated her behavior?

The problem was, no one was reporting on this, or even investigating these questions. The manifesto had been given to the FBI for review by their behavioral experts in Quantico, Virginia. When people called for its release, the FBI claimed that would be up to the Metro Nashville Police Department. That was met with skepticism, however, given the FBI's record of prevarication over the last few years, including the multiple lies surrounding the Trump/Russia investigation and the infamous forgery of the Steele dossier.

At the time of this writing, the public has not seen the manifesto and is likely never to do so. A toxicology report on the deceased assailant has been released but does not include any measure of testosterone or anti-depressant levels the young woman might have had in her body.

Why the strange omissions?

Possibly because elevated levels might explain why this young medically transitioning woman had turned into a rage killer murdering six people and intending to kill more, and might therefore cast the transgender movement in a bad light. That would be politically undesirable to the political ruling class and its media supporters.

But correcting this omission would be key if we genuinely wanted to save lives.

Something of a stalemate has occurred, leaving the city of Nashville, indeed the state of Tennessee, in a difficult, unresolved situation that some say would affect the rapid growth that had earned it, for a while anyway, the title of "It City."

I am not so sure. Events like this, which seem at first glance to be cataclysmic, tend to dissolve in the next news cycle, or perhaps over the next several news cycles.

As for the refugee flow—given the recent mayoral election in Chicago, with Brandon Johnson (a former public school teacher and union organizer who tends to have more sympathy for criminals than their victims) defeating former public schools CEO Paul Vallas (who campaigned on public safety for the bloody streets of that city), not to mention continued mayhem in New York, Los Angeles, San Francisco, and many other blue-state redoubts—it is highly unlikely to stop. ∎

ACKNOWLEDGMENTS

The author would like to thank all those—some whose names appear in this book and others whose don't—for graciously answering my endless questions about their migrations from blue to red. He also thanks Roger Kimball and his "gang" at Encounter who have so faithfully and professionally squired a onetime fiction writer through now three nonfiction books. And finally, as always, he expresses his undying love for his wife Sheryl and daughter Madeleine for putting up with the inevitable mood swings that come with writing. He also thanks Sheryl, again as always, for being his first and indispensable editor. And Rocky Top, don't worry. Your secret is safe with me.